GW01186516

Spinning & Weaving — a practical guide

The lamb's grandmother provided the wool for this jersey

Spinning & Weaving — a practical guide

Eileen Hobden

Photographs S. L. Hobden

ERRATA

Page 14	Caption 6. For "shortwool" read "longwool".
Page 18	Picture is upside down. As printed longwools shown are: Jacob, Wensleydale X Jacob, Wensleydale.
Page 19	Caption 11 should read "Champion Welsh Mountain sheep *with* a good clean fleece.
Page 29	Picture 23 is upside down. As it is printed, the *bottom* yarn is "first try".
Page 52	Caption 49 refers to the bottom picture opposite. Caption 50 to the top picture.
Page 56	Caption 53 refers to the bottom picture and Caption 54 to the top one.

Bishopsgate Press Ltd.
37 Union Street, London, SE1 1SE

© 1985 Bishopsgate Press Ltd.

ISBN 0 900 873 68 X (Cased)
0 900 873 72 8 (Limp)

All enquiries and requests relevant to this title should be sent to the publisher, Bishopsgate Press Ltd., 37 Union Street, London, SE1 1SE

Printed by Whitstable Litho Ltd., Millstrood Road, Whitstable, Kent.

Contents

Introduction

There are many ways of producing handspun yarn. The fleece may be carded, combed, or simply prepared in the hand for spinning by the method which best suits the fleece and the spinner.

Wool can be spun from hand carded rolags in the traditional way, but do not give up the idea of spinning simply because you find carding a painful chore. Excellent yarns can be spun without the use of hand carders.

Even a spinning wheel is not essential. If space is limited, use a spindle. If you make your own spindle, there is no need to buy equipment of any kind. Improvise with whatever you find around you.

You may go to the other extreme, collecting different wheels, skein winders and carders, until the house begins to look like a museum of spinning implements.

The important thing is to enjoy your spinning.

Although most spinners like the thought of sitting at a wheel, the simple spindle has its advantages.

My introduction to the spindle came from sheer necessity. We were in a remote part of Scotland in cold, wet weather, and the car was waiting for spare parts. I made a stick-and-potato spindle and picked up oddments of wool left after sheep-shearing. By being selective in the wool used, I found it easy to spin from teased out locks, and the result was surprisingly successful. A crofter's wife lent some knitting needles (fine "wires" for knitting socks) and soon it was possible to brave the elements in warm gloves and hat. The next day, of course, the weather improved.

Carry a spindle in your bag, and you are ready to try out any fleece which seems interesting. If you spin as you go along, you may begin to feel like the Pied Piper, as you are followed by an interested audience!

For anyone interested in collage or any decorative needlework, a spindle is a boon for making a few yards of yarn for some special effect.

Your handspun wool helps you to be really creative in a number of crafts — rug-making, knitting, crochet, weaving, even lace-making. For those who like to work in miniature, fabrics can be created with patterns in the correct proportions for dressing costume dolls.

When first using handspun, choose simple designs, and build on those as you get to know the characteristics of your yarns, so that they show off at their best. Far too many spinners seem to lose their inspiration when they use their wool. I hope the ideas in this book will help them to make handspun articles to be proud of. It should be a pleasure to use your own wool, as it is to spin it.

Your choice of wheel is a personal one. Take your time, and see as many as possible before deciding which to buy. It must be right for you, and for the yarn you want to spin. If you have made the right choice, you have a friend for life!

Your spinning may even lead to other interests. In our case it resulted in our keeping Jacob sheep, bred for the quality of their wool. We also have the descendents of a Jacob crossed with a Wensleydale, with interesting wool for the handspinner — long, silky, and coloured. Spinning is liable to take over your life!

My husband, Stephen, is in charge of the sheep, and he does the shearing. Numbers are severely restricted by lack of grazing land, but we have an impressive collection of rosettes from shows, and one of our ram lambs was good enough to get a "First" at the Royal Show.

Now both of us sit spinning when time allows, and the items illustrated in this book are made from our handspun yarns. Stephen took all the photographs, too, so it has been a combined operation.

The Fleece

Wool acts as an insulator, trapping many tiny pockets of still air amongst its fibres. It can absorb up to a third of its weight of moisture without feeling wet, and heat is given off when water is drawn in, so that woollen clothes are comfortable to wear in a damp climate.

In comparison with its thickness wool is tough and elastic and there are wools suitable for everything from light gossamer materials to hardwearing fabrics.

Each fibre is covered with overlapping scales, rather like roof tiles. On short wooled sheep the scales are short and very close. On long wooled fleece they are longer and flatter, reflecting the light to give the characteristic lustre of long wool.

On close examination it will be seen that short fine wools have many tiny waves or "crimps" and long wools have much longer waves. The crimp gives the wool its typical resilience; the closer the crimp the more springy is the yarn produced. Short crimpy wools bulk up considerably after spinning and washing, giving the yarn a feeling of warmth. Long wools make a heavier, more solid thread compared with the lightweight airy yarn spun from highly crimped fibres. Very fine wools may have so many crimps to the inch they are difficult to see, and some rough hill sheep have coarse fleece with scarcely a crimp. They often have a high proportion of kemp —short, brittle, chalky white hollow fibres, which break easily and do not absorb dye in the same way as wool. Kemp is a characteristic of Harris tweed, but should be avoided in wool for knitting unless a "whiskery" yarn is required. Kemp reduces the wearing qualities of a woollen material, as the dry brittle fibres continually break off, leaving "bald" patches where the fabric is rubbed.

Quality and Grading

In the description of sheep's wool, along with the staple length and fleece weight, a quality number or "count" is quoted. This originated in the spinning trade, and refers to the number of 560 yd hanks which could be produced from a pound of wool, so the higher the number, the finer the wool. Fine fleeces, like Southdown and Shetland are 56s—60s, and at the coarse end of the scale Scottish Blackface, Swaledale and Herdwick are 28s to 32s. The qualities most suitable for hand spinning are in the 46s to 56s range. Fibres finer than this are often short, but very soft, and for an experienced spinner well worth the time and effort needed. Merino wool (not produced in Britain as the climate is unsuitable) is much finer than any British wool, and some very special wool is now produced in Victoria, Australia from Saxon Merino sheep. They have been bred for their superfine wool, and get V.I.P. treatment, on a balanced diet, and living indoors in single pens. They wear dust jackets so that their wool is not wasted by being soiled or weakened by exposure to sunlight. The wool produced is very much like cashmere, and is known as Natural Sharlea. Such fine wools need very careful handling at every stage, and are for luxury items, not for everyday wear.

Wools coarser than 46s can be spun for furnishing fabrics and for hardwearing outer garments. Many have an interesting character making them attractive for handspinning.

Fleece for Handspinning

Many handspinners begin their hobby after collecting scraps of wool from the fields, but to make a satisfactory yarn the choice of fleece is important.

Sheep produce wool in a great range of quality, length, softness and fineness. It may be from 1½″ to 18″ (4cm to 45cm) long, and the resulting yarn may make a soft shawl of cobweb fineness or a hardwearing carpet.

As there are well over forty breeds of British sheep, plus local variations and crosses, there is a wide choice.

Beginners should avoid the extremes — the longest, the shortest and finest — but in the middle range of quality and length there is enough variety of suit any handspinner. For woollen spinning a 3″ — 4″ (8cm to 10cm) staple is ideal, and for worsted type spinning, 5″ to 7″ (12cm to 17cm). The fleece should be of medium fineness, with an "open" texture, so that it can to teased (separated out) without difficulty. It should be clean, free from thorns, grass seeds and twigs. It can then be spun with the minimum of preparation.

2. *Longwools. Wensleydale, Romney and Devon and Cornwall*

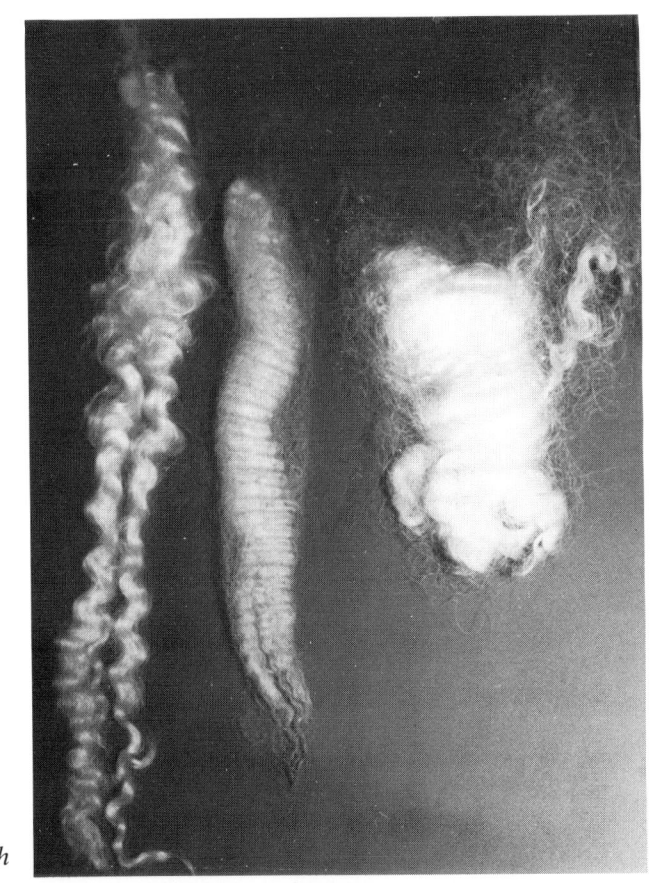

3. *Shortwools. Shetland and Polwarth (from Falkland Islands)*

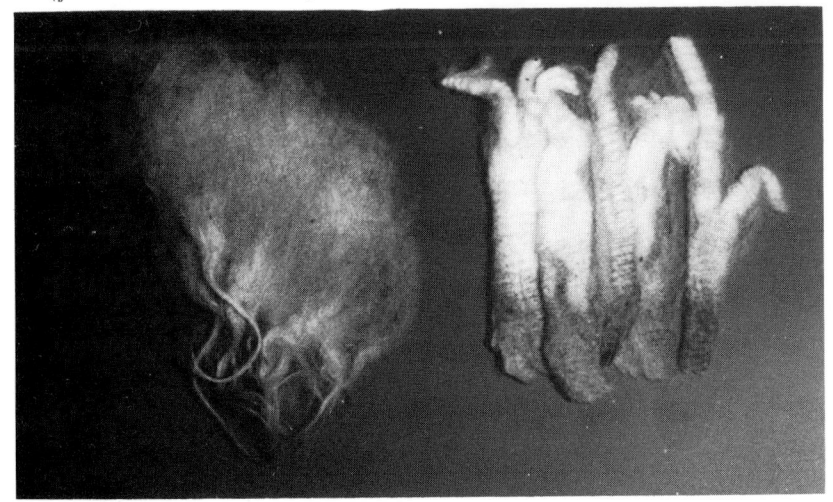

Choosing a Fleece

It takes years of experience to judge the quality of a fleece, so take the advice of experts. A handspinner may be available to help you make the right choice, or the British Wool Marketing Board, who grade wool from the whole country, can find you a fleece suitable for your requirements. (See chart p. 112).

It is a great advantage to choose your fleece when the sheep is still wearing it, so that you can see the quality and length of wool over the whole body.

To see wool of many kinds at close quarters visit a local market, or walk through the sheep lines at an agricultural show. After the judging the owners will be happy to tell you all about the fleece. You may find a "small" shepherd who keeps so few sheep that fleeces can be bought direct from the source, instead of through the Wool Board.

The suitability of a fleece for spinning may be affected by the location of the flock, as well as the type of wool. Some sheep stay beautifully clean, when others of the same breed become clogged with mud, matted with brambles or rubbed bare on fences.

Wool classed as "white" comes in a range of cream and ivory shades, and it is not always easy to judge the colour of the finished yarn.

The ancestors of our modern sheep were coloured, and in spite of selective breeding, coloured fibres still appear in "white" fleeces, particularly in breeds with coloured faces and legs. Look for these fibres. It is irritating to spend time spinning what it is hoped will be white wool, and after washing it is found to be flecked with grey.

Quality varies within breeds, and even in one flock. The wool can be affected by adverse weather conditions, poor feeding, lambing difficulties, antibiotics and other factors.

4. *Sheep at Haywards Heath Market*

5. *Suffolk Down–a shortwool sheep*

When new wool begins to grow in the spring there is a definite "rise" where the new clean wool emerges, and ideally the wool is shorn between the new growth and the old. Just before the rise the fibres are often weaker, sometimes broken, a survival of the natural "moult" of the ancestors of the sheep. A similar weakness may occur as a result of illness or stress.

The little Soay sheep, (a primitive breed), sheds its old coat when spring pasture improves and new growth begins.

Shetland sheep were plucked, or "rooed", when they began to lose their old wool, so that the soft undercoat could be kept separately from the outer hairy covering.

The first clip of a shearling (a sheep just over a year old, also known as a hogget, hog or teg) is the best of all for handspinning.

Certain breeds are favourites with handspinners, but there may be unfamiliar breeds and crosses in any particular area which are equally good.

A clean, silky Romney (Kent) fleece can be a joy to spin, and requires very little preparation. It is equally useful for a learner or an experienced spinner.

6. Romney–a shortwool sheep

Some of the hill breeds produce good wool for handspinning. The Lonk, for instance, living in the Pennines between Yorkshire and Lancashire, has good wool, very easily prepared and spun, washing to a clear white, and a good fleece is soft enough for knitting jerseys and cardigans, but strong enough to keep in shape with everyday wear.

The Clun Forest sheep has a dense, fine fleece of uniform quality, its staple length of 3″ – 4″ (8 – 10 cm) making it ideal for wool spinning. This applies to the "Down" breeds — Hampshire, Suffolk, Dorset, Oxford, Shropshire, etc. More careful preparation may be needed compared with longer staple wools but the production of a soft springy yarn makes is a worthwhile exercise.

The finest of the "Down" breeds is the Southdown. Its length, 2″ – 3″ (5 – 8 cm) makes it unsuitable for a learner, but its soft texture, elasticity and lightweight "handle" make it attractive to anyone prepared to take the necessary trouble.

Lustrous long wools like the Teeswater and Wensleydale make interesting spinning projects for combing rather than carding, and the longest and heaviest of them all, the Lincoln, when well prepared, can be spun into very strong yarn.

Coloured Fleeces

Many spinners prefer to use naturally coloured fleece, rather than use dyes, and there are many shades available in a number of breeds and crosses.

Black Welsh Mountain, though rather short for a learner is good for wool spinning. Jacobs wool is particularly suitable for a beginner, because the possibilities of colour variation can almost guarantee an "interesting" yarn. Herdwick spins easily. It is coarse and often kempy, but makes hardwearing clothes or rugs, and the colours can be varied by using wool from sheep of different ages — the wool gets lighter as the animal grows older.

Jacobs crossed with sheep of other breeds usually have coloured lambs and the mixed characteristics of their parents can give wool of different length, lustre, fineness and softness. The dark lock in Ill. 9 shows its descent from Wensleydale (left) and Jacob (right).

For the experienced spinner there are many soft shades of Shetland wool and in many flocks of normally white sheep there are a few with black or brown fleeces.

7. Jacob and Welsh Mountain sheep in North Wales

Weathering bleaches the tips of the wool, so by shearing time a dark sheep may appear pale coloured. The original colour comes to light when the wool is shorn.

You may prefer to learn to spin before buying a whole fleece. Sorted fleece can be bought by the pound.

Some of the "living museum" woollen mills sell ready carded fleece for handspinners. This is an excellent arrangement as a learner can spin wool of different kinds before deciding which will be best to buy in quantity. Also, buying wool prepared for spinning reduces the number of skills to be learned all at once.

Check list for choice of fleece

Is it the required length, strength, softness, fineness and lustre for the purpose?

Is it clean enough? Bad stains may not wash out and it is difficult to judge the true colour of very dirty wool. A clean fleece saves hours of preparation time.

Is it matted, where new wool has grown through the old, and felted into the fleece? A badly matted fleece cannot be pulled apart without damaging the fibres even further.

Are there "foreign bodies" (twigs, etc) which will be a nuisance when preparing for spinning?

Is there a weakness in the staple, which gives way when a lock is pulled between the fingers?

Is there much kemp amongst the wool?

In a "white" fleece, is there a scattering of dark fibres?

If a high proportion is not worth spinning, or if many hours will be wasted trying to tease and card dirty, matted wool, a "cheap" fleece is not a bargin.

8. Sheep and shepherd warmly clad in the snow

9. Longwools. Wensleydales, Wensleydales and Jacob, Jacob

10. *Jacob sheep with fleece in excellent condition*

11. *Champion Welsh Mountain sheep a good clean fleece*

Sorting a Fleece

A rolled fleece is secured with a twisted tie of wool pulled up, usually from the neck end, so that it holds the fleece in a compact bundle. In some areas the tie is made from the tail end, so that the poorest fleece is on the outside.

To examine the whole fleece, carefully free the band and unroll the package.

A large area is needed. If possible work out of doors, spreading an old sheet on the ground. If this cannot be done clear a large floor space.

The sides of the fleece are rolled inwards. Open it up carefully and untwist the tie. Decide whether it is from the neck or the tail. If it is the neck be particularly careful, as the best wool is probably in the band. Unroll the fleece and carefully unfold the sides.

Look at the whole fleece and note the variation in quality in different parts.

The fleece may appear lop-sided, as some are shorn with all the belly wool to one side, or there may be half on each side.

Discard anything which is too short or too stained to be of use.

Carefully remove locks of wool from different areas and compare the length, "feel", crimp, fineness, strength and softness.

The quality of a fleece from a healthy, well fed sheep may be uniformly good, except for the legs and tail, and the short belly wool. From a poorer animal only the shoulder wool may be of good quality. The back is often rubbed and worn and sometimes matted.

The wool from under the neck is soft and fine, but shorter. Belly wool, too, is soft, but is short and has little strength. Often it is very dirty.

Poorer quality wool from the back end can be washed and used for learning to spin.

When sorting the fleece, keep a number of cardboard boxes handy to take the different grades. Take the poorest wool first. Anything considered too dirty or stained can be soaked in water to make liquid manure, and very short fibres can be washed and used for stuffing toys.

Continue to remove wool in ascending order of quality, and label each box. Fleece can also be stored in woven sacks, but not in plastic. Newspaper parcels, clearly labelled with quality, type, weight and date, can be used for storage, and the printers ink is considered to be a moth deterrent.

Good sorting is essential to avoid uneven shrinkage and felting

12. Unroll fleece carefully

13. Unfold sides

as well as to achieve uniform spinning. If wools with different amounts of crimp are used in a garment there will be a loss of shape. Uneven tension in weaving can be caused by variations in stretch of different fibres.

If a large quantity of matching wool is required and a single grade of the sorted fleece is insufficient, it may be necessary to mix two qualities. However, it must be a uniform mix, carefully done when the wool is teased, to produce a yarn of even quality.

A newly shorn fleece is much easier to handle than one which has been rolled and stored for a long time. Best of all is a fleece sorted immediately after shearing, without being rolled as a whole fleece. Whenever possible, do the sorting before the grease is set and hard. Otherwise place the fleece where it can "warm up" before handling it.

In addition to sorting for quality, divide Jacob fleece according to colour— all light, all dark and mixed.

14. Jacob fleece ready for sorting

Preparation of Fleece

First of all, decide whether the fleece should be washed before it is spun. The fibres must be easily separated, or drafting will be difficult. Grease becomes more solid with storage, and washing can make an apparently "difficult" fleece easy to handle.

However, if the fleece looks clean, and teases out easily, spin it "in the grease." A good fleece, particularly if it is newly shorn, needs so little preparation for spinning, it seems a pity to spend time washing it.

A wash in clear water removes the dirt but not the grease. The lanolin in the fleece helps the washing process.

Remember that a combination of damp, warmth and friction will felt the wool, so agitate the fleece as little as possible. Avoid temperature shocks when washing. There is no need to remove all the grease. The aim is to make the fleece easy to handle. Deal with small quantities at a time (8oz to 1 lb) until you feel confident to tackle a whole fleece.

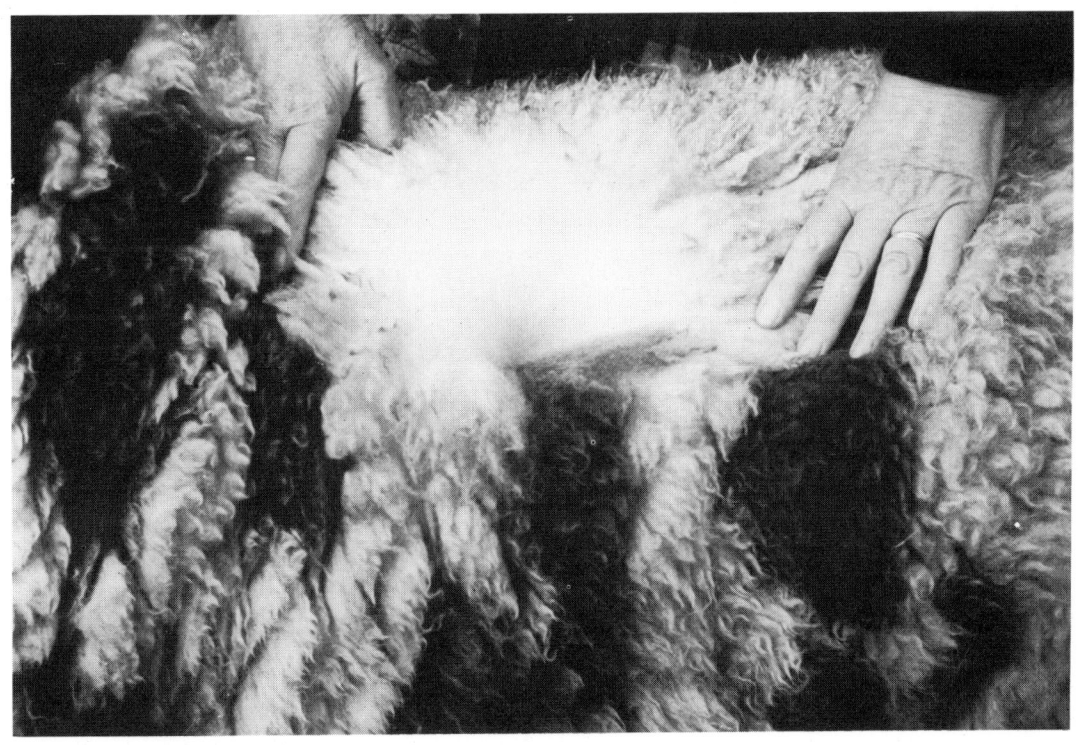

15. A clean fleece which can be spun "in the grease"

First soak the wool in plain warm water, soft water if possible.

Using soap flakes or a mild detergent, prepare a bowl of suds and add the squeezed out wool. A surprising amount of dirt will have been left behind in the first bowl of water. Leave fleece in the suds for several hours, then rinse in warm water, being careful not to rub, stretch or twist the fleece. Never run water from the tap directly on to the fleece. Be careful when lifting the wet wool. Support it underneath. Rinse in clean water again, then squeeze out surplus moisture. Never leave wet fleece hanging around. Roll in a towel, or give a quick spin, with the fleece in an old pillowcase, then dry on a rack, to that air can circulate, well away from direct sunlight.

There should be enough grease left in the wool to spin without the addition of extra oil. It may not be necessary to use suds in the washing process — the original soak in plain water may leave the fleece clean enough to handle. The proportions of waxes of different kinds vary so much in different breeds that it is impossible to treat them all alike. A higher temperature may be necessary to soften the grease, particularly in some long wool fleeces, but this could damage more delicate fleeces. Experience is the best teacher!

If the wool feels too dry for spinning, spray with a mixture of equal parts oil and water. Olive oil or neatsfoot oil can be used. Some cooking oils are suitable, but experiment with a small quantity first, to make sure it washes out easily. Leave the re-oiled wool wrapped in an old towel for a few hours before spinning, but do not do too much in advance, or the oil may go rancid.

Spinning your first yarn — with a spindle

To produce really good yarn you need fleece which has been carefully sorted, but the odds and ends picked up in the fields provide the raw material for making a continuous thread on a spindle.

Avoid very short fleece, as anything less than 3″ is difficult for a beginner, and try to find springy wool, which still retains some of the natural oils.

If you are lucky enough to have a whole fleece, use the rougher parts for your first efforts at spinning. Save the better wool until you are more expert. Rough hairy wool draws out and "holds" easily when spun and makes an interesting yarn for a beginner.

The spindle is a good introduction to spinning, so that you understand the basic techniques before attempting to use a wheel. By experimenting with a home made spindle you can decide on the size and weight which suits you best. Later you can buy or make a more artistic version, and for anyone who travels, collecting spindles of different kinds can become an interesting hobby.

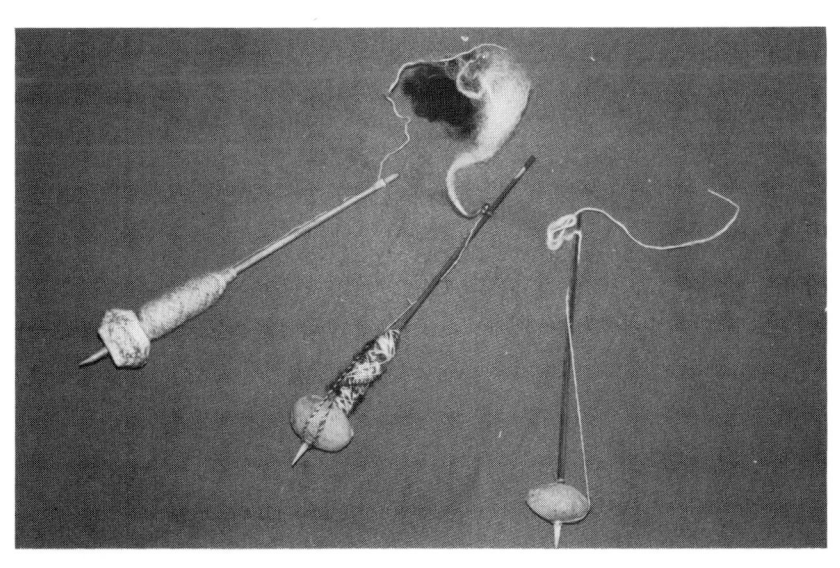

16. Home made spindles

Making the Spindle

All you need is a straight smooth stick about a foot in length, and something to act as a whorl — the weight which balances the spindle as it twists. Use a small potato, a lump of clay, or anything handy which is fairly symmetrical and about an ounce in weight. A lightweight cotton reel can be built up with layers of paper mache into a whorl of the right weight. A little gummed tape, or cotton bandage, may be needed to thicken the stick slightly to fit into a cotton reel, if you use 1/4" dowel.

Sharpen one end of the stick and push it through the whorl so that about one inch protrudes. Round off the other end, then make an upward sloping notch near the top.

Tie one end of a yard length of wool (rather hairy knitting wool works well) to the stick just above the whorl. Wind a few turns round the stick, then take the thread down, round the point at the base, then up to the top, securing it in the notch with a half hitch. Your spindle is now ready to use.

Preparing the Fleece

Take a lock of wool, and holding the tips firmly between the 3rd and 4th fingers of one hand, part the strands at the other end. Turn the wool end to end, and holding the teased out fibres, separate the tips in the same way. The strands should be lying roughly parallel, and most of the dirt will have been loosened, so that the fibres draw out easily.

The prepared fibres should be placed in a shallow box or basket, with the tips all facing the same way, so that they can be picked up easily. Tease out enough fleece to keep you supplied while you spin.

There are other methods of preparing fleece, using combs and carders, as you will see later in the book, but for your first attempts at spinning the above method is simple and effective. If you are lucky in your choice of fleece this simple preparation will be all that is necessary for fine spinning, too.

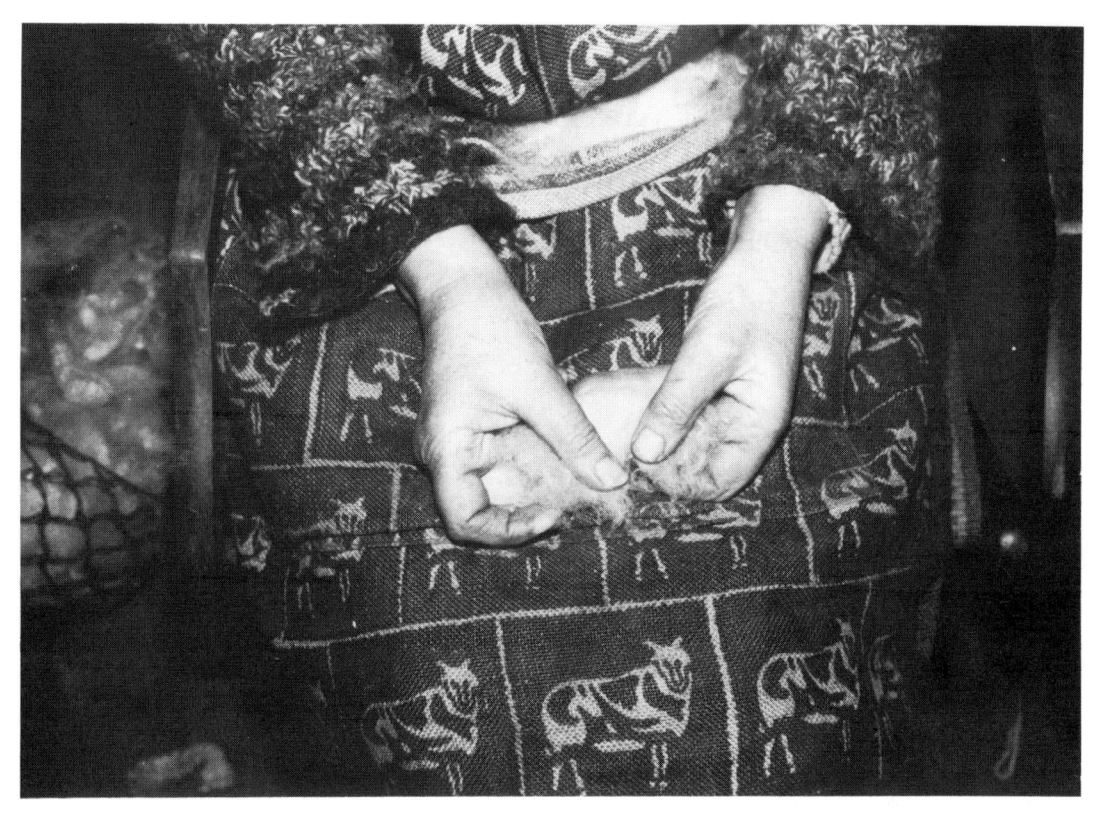

17. Preparing the fleece–teasing

Spinning on the Spindle

Pick up the spindle with one hand, holding the end of the wool tied to it. Take some teased wool in the other hand, and draw out a few strands, overlapping the wool from the spindle a few inches from the end. (Ill. 18)

Hold the fibres firmly over the wool with finger and thumb, and with the finger and thumb of the other hand twist the spindle clockwise. The "spin" will run up the wool and drawn-out strands as far as the point where it is firmly held. (Ill. 19)

While the spindle is still turning move up the spinning hand and grip the newly spun yarn drawing out more fibres with the other hand. Grip again with that hand and give the spindle another twist so that the spin runs up into the newly drawn out fibres. (Ill. 20)

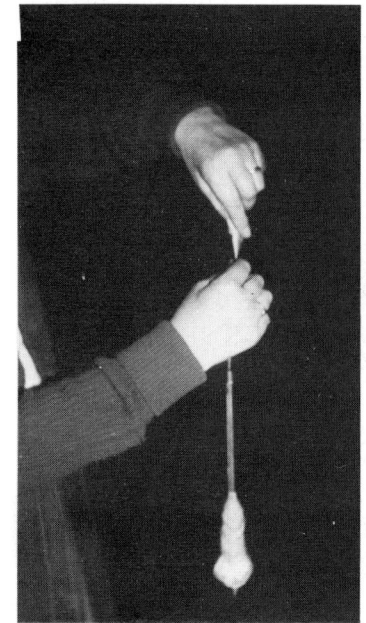 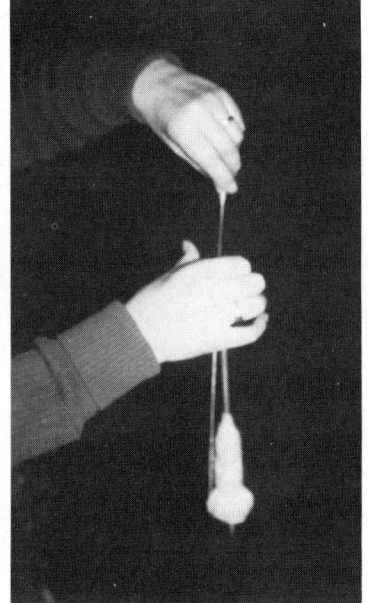 

18. Joining new fibres   *19. Twisting spindle*   *20. Drawing out*

Continue in this way, giving another twist to the spindle when necessary to keep it turning in the same direction. If it stops and then reverses, the yarn will untwist and break. The strength of the yarn depends on the amount of twist.

If at first you find it difficult to keep an eye on the spindle as well as controlling the yarn, let somebody else keep the spindle going while you concentrate on making the thread. When you feel more confident you can take over the spindle, too.

Practice is needed to judge the amount of twist, and to draw out the right number of fibres. The thread will no doubt break from time to time. If so, lay the last few inches of yarn from the spindle over your fibre supply and carry on as at the beginning, when you joined the first threads on to the wool on the spindle.

At first it is an achievement to spin a foot of unbroken yarn, then suddenly the process becomes easier, the spindle reaches the floor at the end of a length of yarn, and it is time for "winding on".

Do not let the yarn go slack when you stop to wind on, or it will twist back onto itself. Holding it taut, wind the thread in a figure of

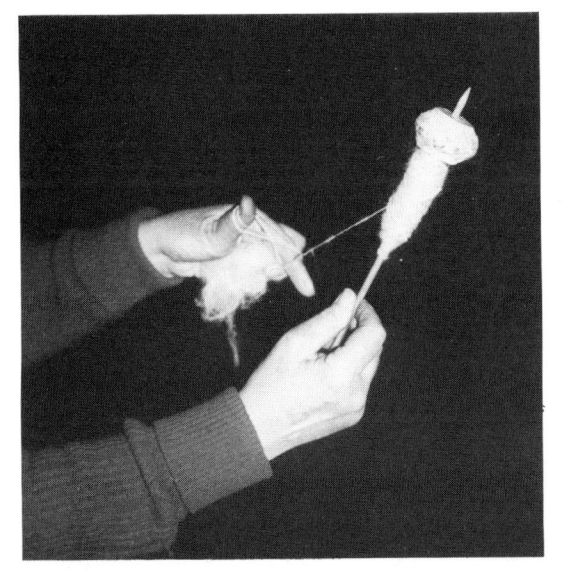

21. Winding on

22. Hitching into notch to start again

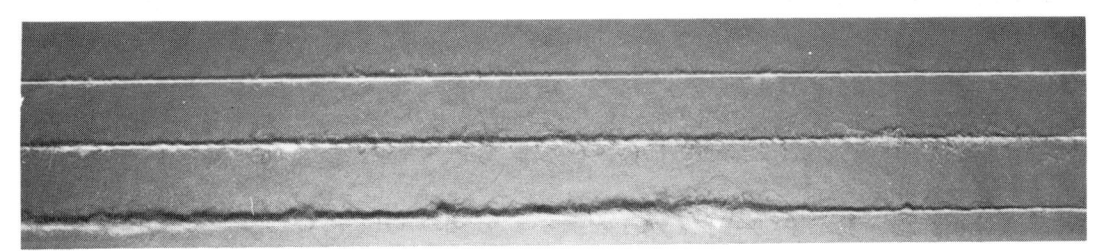

23. Progress in spinning–top yarn is first try

eight on thumb and fingers from the fleece end, then unhook the wool from the notch and from the point at the base, and wind the yarn on to the stick just above the whorl, leaving enough yarn to go round the point and up into the notch as before. By winding it neatly and keeping the growing ball of wool low on the spindle it will balance well and should slide off easily when completed. (Ill. 21, 22)

Do not worry at first about the quality of the yarn. Aim at making a continuous thread, until gradually your hands work to a rhythm of spinning, drawing out, holding, changing the grip, and winding on.

At first parts of the yarn will be overspun, and there will be "slubs" of unspun fibres, but with practice you will be able to control the thickness and the amount of twist.

Skeining

The wool needs to be washed after it has been removed from the spindle. It should be made into a skein, and if you have no special equipment this can be done round the backs of two chairs placed so that once round the skein is 1½ yds or 2yds to make it easy to calculate the total length of wool.

Remember to remove the length of wool put on the spindle at the beginning. After your first try, the spindle can be started with a length of handspun, then the whole of the ball can go into the skein. Tie the skein in several places to keep the threads in order. The ties should be loose, and in a figure of eight, as in illustration 24, so that the water can penetrate into the wool. Otherwise there will be dirty greasy patches under the ties. Washing instructions can be found on page 72.

When you stop spinning the loose yarn beyond the notch will untwist, so whenever you pick up the spindle to start again, give it a twist immediately so that the yarn can take the weight, before joining newly drawn out fibres.

Although using a spindle seems slow compared with spinning on a wheel, the simpler version has its advantages. Spindles can be carried anywhere, and without great expense or storage room you can have a collection of spindles of various weights and sizes suited to a variety of yarns. When the Romans came to Britain they reported back that the people here could "spin wool so fine it was comparable to a spider's web", and the Britons had no spinning Wheels!

Illustration 23 shows the progress from the first uneven thread to a smooth fine yarn.

24. Figure of eight tie on skein

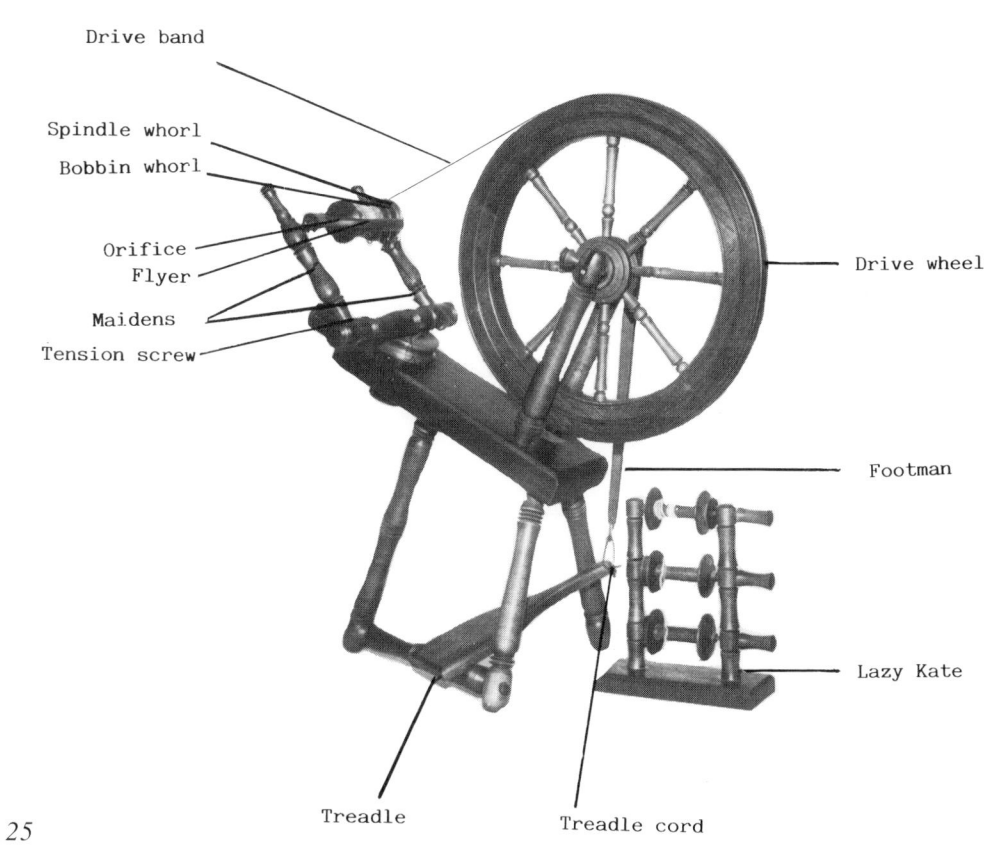

Drive band

Spindle whorl

Bobbin whorl

Orifice

Flyer

Maidens

Tension screw

Drive wheel

Footman

Lazy Kate

Treadle

Treadle cord

25

The Spinning Wheel

The wheel performs as a spindle, but winds on the yarn, too. The spindle is held horizontally, usually between two supports known as maidens. A drive band operated by the action of treadle pulls the wheel around, and as the spindle whorl is very much smaller, it revolves much faster than the drive wheel.

The spun yarn goes through the orifice in the end of the spindle, over the hooks on the U-shaped flyer, and on to the bobbin. On a double band wheel the bobbin, with a smaller whorl than the spindle pulley, revolves more quickly than the spindle. A single band wheel, with a brake on the bobbin (a Scotch tension wheel), has the bobbin revolving more slowly than the spindle. In either case the difference in speed between the bobbin and spindle pulley allows the yarn to wind on.

26. Modern Scotch tension wheel

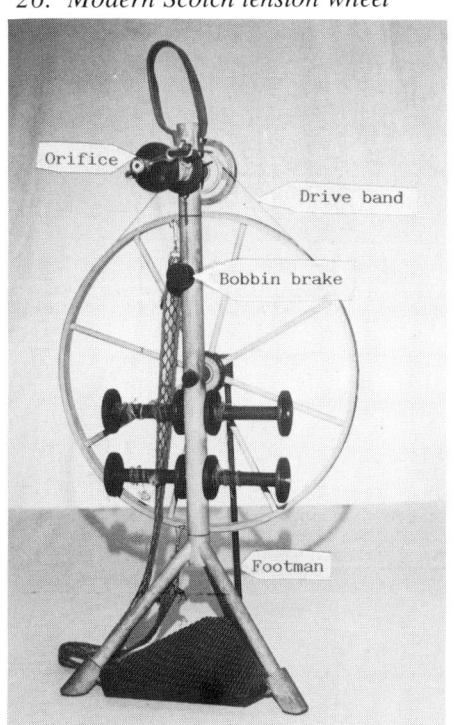

27. Close up Scotch tension wheel

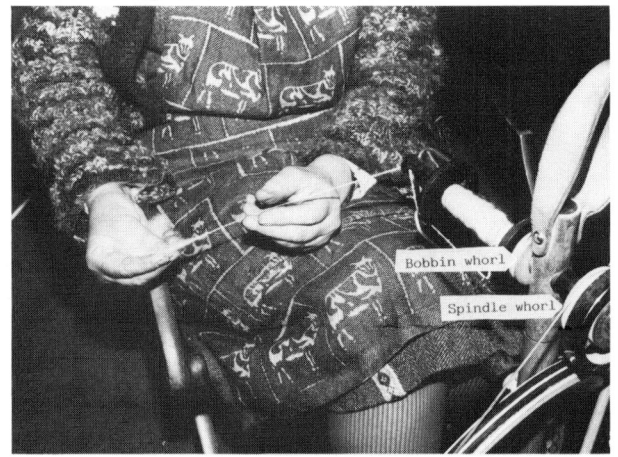

The Double Band Wheel

The "double band" wheel has a continuous cord going round the drive wheel, the spindle whorl, the drive wheel again, and the bobbin pulley. It is the ratio between the diameters of the drive wheel and spindle pulley which determines how many revolutions of the spindle are made for each turn of the drive wheel. This is the "drive ratio".

The difference in diameter of the bobbin pulley and spindle whorl determines the rate of winding on to the bobbin. The smaller pulley on the bobbin makes it revolve more quickly, and the yarn winds on to the bobbin in the same direction as the wheel turns. The band controls both the traction of the drive wheel and the winding on of the yarn. A single tension screw adjusts the band. There may be two spindle whorls, one larger than the other, to adjust the winding on.

28. Useful in limited space–an unusual fold flat wheel

29. A sturdy efficient modern wheel

The Scotch Tension Wheel

There is a single drive band around the spindle whorl and drive wheel, so the ratio between the two determines the number of revolutions of the spindle to each turn of the drive wheel. The band should have good contact in the groove to work efficiently.

A separate cord goes round the bobbin groove to a peg fixed conveniently so that it can be turned to adjust the braking effect on the bobbin. This makes the bobbin revolve more slowly than the flyer, and the yarn winds on in the reverse direction from that of the drive wheel. The cord for the bobbin tension can be softer and finer than the drive band, for fine adjustment of the brake.

Choosing a Wheel

The choice of a wheel depends on personal preference, as well as the type of spinning to be undertaken.

A double band wheel with a generously sized drive wheel is excellent for the traditional long draw and for plying. Usually it has a pleasant treadling action.

On a Scotch tension wheel the yarn winds on more quickly, and the wheel tension can be left undisturbed, with slight adjustments to the bobbin brake only. Probably this type of wheel is easier for spinning bulky wools, although many double band wheels can be adapted if necessary.

Some new versions made with the benefit of modern engineering, are more efficient than traditional wheels. Make sure you buy a wheel which has been made to use regularly, not as a decoration for the ingle nook.

Upright or Horizontal?

If floor space has to be considered, and easy transport, the answer might be an upright wheel, but there are compact horizontal wheels which take up very little space.

Usually the orifice on a horizontal wheel is at a convenient height so that the wool on the bobbin is always in view, not hidden by the end of the spool, but some upright wheels have well placed bobbins.

A large wheel for fast spinning is more likely to be of the horizontal type, but some upright wheels have a high drive ratio.

30. *Small antique flaxwheel–pretty rather than practical*

What to look for when buying a wheel

If you are a learner, take a spinner with you, and some prepared fleece. See how the wheel works spinning thick soft yarn and fine yarn.

If you are buying a wheel already assembled, see it working, in the workshop if possible. It must be well finished, not just for the appearance, but for efficiency. Small firms often produce wheels with excellent finish and individual character. Every wheel is lovingly made as a separate creation and the maker aims at producing something to be proud of. A craftsman who is a spinner will make sure the wheel really works well.

For reasons of economy, many spinners buy wheels which arrive in kit form, to be assembled at home. Some of these are very good, but you may be unlucky and get a wheel with some badly fitting parts. The help of an experienced spinner may be needed to check the assembly. Something slightly out of place can make a wheel unusable, yet probably the fault can easily be corrected.

Old spinning wheels were often made without glue or screws, and some tend to fall apart in a warm, dry house. Often the plainer old wheels are more efficient than the drawing room versions. The grooves in the spindle pulley may be worn, making the whorl smaller than the original size. If everything else is satisfactory this can be corrected by wrapping a few layers of linen thread into the groove.

Check list for all wheels

Moving parts must work easily. There should be no wobble in the wheel. Does it rattle anywhere?

Try treadling. Is it an effort? Is the treadle plate a comfortable size? If both feet will go on it, so much the better. At its lowest position the treadle should not slope downwards from the pivoting points. Check this. Is there room for the foot on the treadle, not just the toes? The treadle was usually pivoted at the front, but many modern wheels have a heel-toe action which gives much better control. A few wheels have double treadles (like an old harmonium) but many are so heavy and clumsy they are of little advantage.

Check the **alignment** — the drive wheel must be in line with the spindle and bobbin grooves.

31. Battered old Brazilian Wheel

32. Another crudely made Brazilian wheel

The **drive band** and **wheel grooves** are important. There must be enough friction between band and groove to work the wheel. On a double band wheel the bobbin groove should be deeper than the spindle groove.

Look at the **tension screw.** On a double drive band wheel, this is often a wood screw controlled from the end of the table. Make sure the screw will hold at any point. There must be no jerky movements or exact adjustment will be impossible.

On any kind of tensioner, make sure it can be "finely tuned".

Single band wheels usually have two adjusting points, for the bobbin brake and the drive hand; however, some modern wheels have a flexible belt needing no attention, so the brake band only needs to be adjusted. Very slight movement must be possible on the brake band. Check this carefully — some wheels have insecure brake pegs which could slip during spinning. Occasionally the brake is in the flyer and the drive on the bobbin.

The **orifice** should be of suitable size. About $3/10''$ – $1/2''$ (1cm – 1.25cm) is ample for most spinning. The orifice on an old wheel may be very small, suitable only for fine spinning. An alternative spindle pulley may be available for spinning bulky wool. If your wheel has a large orifice and large bobbins this can be a useful extra.

Try threading the leader through the orifice. Is it easy, or will it become a time wasting irritation?

Make sure the **flyer** moves freely and that the arms are wide enough to take a fully loaded bobbin. Are the hooks smooth, and are there sufficient to allow even distribution along the bobbin? A movable eye which slides along the flyer is a great improvement on the usual hooks.

Look at the **bearings** holding the flyer. Traditionally they are leather, and should be firm, not soft. Modern wheels often have bearings of teflon or nylon.

Are the **bobbins** easily removed? Check how bobbin is changed. Sometimes the spindle whorl will pull off, or it may unscrew. Usually it has a left hand thread. Check that it stays firm when the wheel is in use. Look at any movement on maidens when changing the bobbin. Will it loosen with constant use? When re-assembling, make sure the maiden is in its correct position.

Try **all** the bobbins on the spindle shaft, making sure they turn freely. Are they a suitable size for the yarn you hope to spin? A dainty spool which holds only an ounce of wool is useless for chunky spinning. When buying a new wheel buy at least three bobbins, preferably more. An old wheel may have one bobbin only, and spares would have to be specially made.

If the bobbins can be quickly changed without disturbing the tension screw, that is a great advantage, saving time and the possibility of starting off again at a different tension.

Preparation of Fleece for Spinning

The preparation will depend on the length and quality of the fleece and the type of yarn to be spun.

Anything over 3″ long can be combed, or if it is an "easy" fleece, simply opened out in the hand before being spun.

Shorter fibres should be carded, either on hand or drum carders, for a true woollen yarn. Colour blending is most easily managed by carding, too, so it is a skill worth mastering.

Drum carders are available to many spinners and you may find in your area an industrial museum where your fleece can be carded on an old fashioned machine. This can be a great boon if you have a "difficult" fleece, but it is a pity to drum card or machine card a fleece which can easily be prepared by hand. Carding may damage soft fine wools, so make sure the carders used suit the fleece being prepared — fine teeth for fine wools.

An "easy" fleece can be spun after opening up the fibres in the hand as described for spindle spinning. (p. 28)

Simple Combing

Traditional wool combing needs special apparatus and techniques, well described by Peter Teal in his book "Hand Woolcombing and Spinning", but a dog comb can be used to comb locks of wool for spinning. A comb with a handle is the most comfortable type to use.

Holding 2 or 3 locks between thumb and fingers, comb out the tips so that the fibres are separated. Turn over and comb the underside. If necessary, turn the locks round and comb the butt end, too.

Work gently. Usually the aim is to loosen the dirt and free the fibres so that drafting is easy, not to comb out all the short ends, which help to make a warm, airy yarn.

For a yarn of worsted type the short ends are combed out, leaving the long, straightened out fibres to spin into a smooth, compact yarn.

Store the prepared wool with the ends lying the same way to make it easy to pick up when spinning.

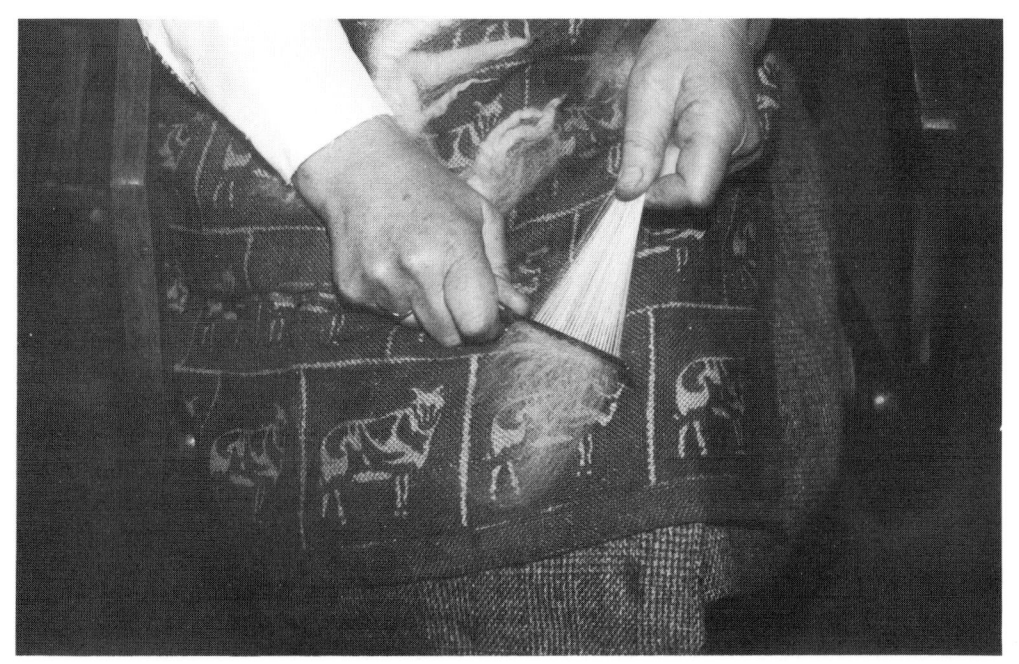

33. Combing tips

34. Completing combing

Carding for Wool Spinning

Carders should be marked L and R so that they are always used in the same hand. When new the teeth are alike on both carders but with use they change slightly and should not be switched from hand to hand.

Using fleece with a staple length of about 3 inches, (8cm), tease out locks of wool thoroughly. Solid lumps of fleece will not card well.

Choose a chair where you can sit comfortably with the left foot firmly on the floor and the right foot under the chair.

Hold the left carder with an underhand grip, teeth upwards, supported on the left knee.

With the right hand place small pieces of teased wool on the hooks drawing them down the carder so that the fibres lie straight, in a thin layer. (Ill. 35)

Holding the right hand carder with an overhand grip, teeth down, push the fibres on the left carder. (Ill. 36)

Comb the wool at the bottom edge first, and gradually work up the lower carder. Use long strokes, so that the top carder is drawn clear of the lower one before making the next stroke. (Ill. 37) Start gently, then repeat more firmly two or three times, transferring most of the wool to the right carder.

With carders upright, facing inwards, right carder supported on knee, left carder above right, brush left carder downwards so that wool is transferred to left carder. Start with left carder high enough to collect the fringe of fibres on edge of right carder. (Ill. 38)

Again brush with right carder as before.

Now transfer to right carder, left carder supported upright on knee, right carder facing and above, stroke down to collect fleece on right carder. (Ill. 39)

Repeat the sequence of brushing and transferring until fleece is uniformly spread and there is an even fringe of wool on the lower. If the fleece was properly teased there should be no seeds or lumpy "noils", but if any show up during carding, pick them out.

To remove the carded fleece for making into rolags, hold carders upright and transfer fleece very lightly, (Ill. 40) then even more lightly back again so that it is loose and curved, ready to be rolled on the back of the carder.

Tip on to the back of one carder, and use the other to flatten the fleece slightly, then roll into a rolag, using the back of the other carder. (Ill. 41) Many spinners prefer to take off the fleece in two

35. Loading carder

36. Brush fibres with right carder

37. Use long stroke

38. Transfer fleece to left carder

layers, making two rolags. As good rolags from fine fleece are no thicker than your thumb, your spinning will benefit if you make two rolags each time. The most common fault is overloading the carders, which leaves some of the fleece inadequately carded,

The idea is to make an air filled spiral of fibres which can be drawn out to make a light yarn. Twist will vary according to the purpose of the yarn, but for the production of a light, soft yarn, quickly spun, there is nothing to beat well made rolags.

Care must be taken not to tear the fibres. Card with a quick, gentle brushing motion, not a strong pull.

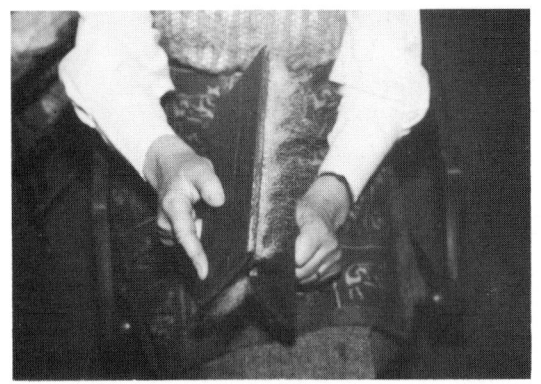

39. Transfer to right carder

40. Lightly remove fleece from carders

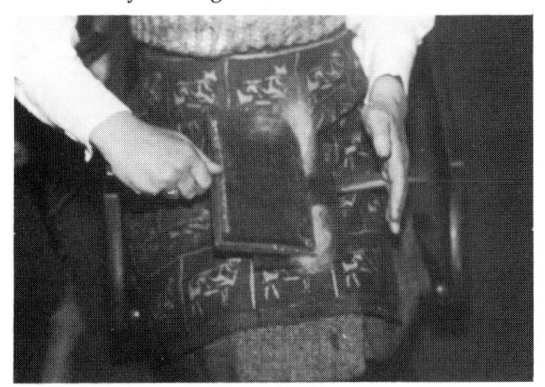

41. Roll fleece between carders

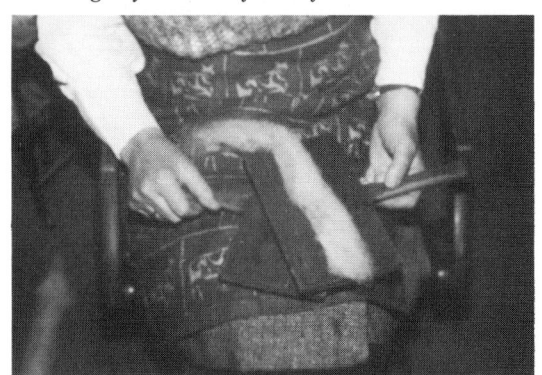

42. Rolag completed

Drum Carders

A drum carder can be a great time saver, but make sure the teeth of the carder suit the fleece to be processed. Fine wool will be damaged by coarse teeth. Very fine fleeces demand gentle treatment, and are better carded by hand.

Clean fleece saves time cleaning the carder, so wash the fleece first, and dry it well.

Thorough teasing is necessary, too, to get good results.

Place teased wool on the tray to feed it into the machine, turning the handle as you work. (Ill. 43) Distribute the wool evenly. Continue to feed in fleece, but do not over fill the carder. About ½oz (15 gm) is a manageable weight for each batt.

Turn the drum to bring the join to the top, and insert a long skewer or knitting needle at the join. Lift up the batt of wool until it breaks. (Ill. 44)

44

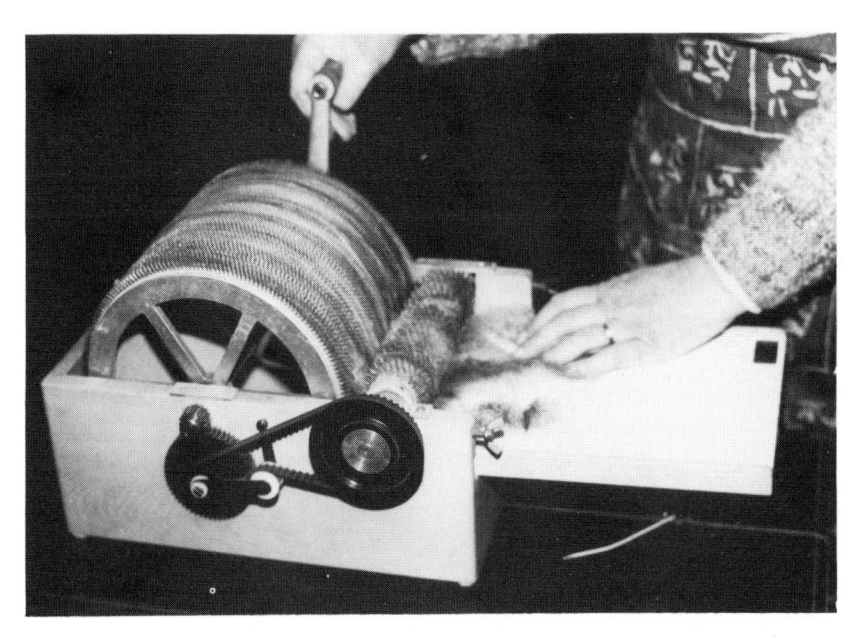

43. Feed teased fleece into carder

44. Lift batt with skewer

45. Turn in reverse direction to remove batt of wool

Turn the handle in the reverse direction, lifting the batt until it comes free. Help with the skewer if necessary. (Ill. 45)

A well made batt will be of even thickness when held up to the light. If not, after removing any small lumps, tear the batt into strips and card it again.

The drum carder is useful for colour blending, either to get an even shade or a variegated effect. When blending a large quantity of wool, check that the proportions of colour are the same throughout.

Clean the carder as you finish each batch. If you use clean wool, it will not take long. Dirty wool quickly clogs up the carder.

There is a long tradition of handspinners using commercially carded or combed fleece. At the beginning of the industrial revolution carding mills supplied hand spinners until spinning machinery took over. Professional combers supplied "tops" for worsted spinning. If you enjoy being a spinner, but don't want to be a comber, too, you are not breaking with tradition!

Spinning

Getting to know the Wheel

If you have never used a spinning wheel, start by treadling only, without trying to spin a yarn.

Having found a chair of a convenient height for operating the wheel, sit facing the orifice (the eye end of the spindle) so that you can work the treadle.

Traditional wheels have the treadle pivoted at the front so that the pressure from the foot must be sufficient to revolve the wheel completely, and a strong push is required to start the wheel. Once it starts revolving a lighter pressure will keep up the momentum.

Many modern wheels have the treadle pivoted for heel and toe action which makes the wheel easier to control. Another device for maintaining momentum is the addition of weights in the rims.

If there is a long tie between the treadle and the footman (the rod connection the crank to the treadle) or if the footman is a cord, special care is needed when treadling. The foot must not be lifted from the treadle or the rhythm will be lost.

To start, give a push with the right hand to turn the wheel clockwise, and treadle, starting with a strong push, and treadle lightly to keep it going. Treadle when the footman reaches its highest point and is beginning to go down. If the right moment is missed, the wheel will reverse. Persevere until without effort the wheel runs smoothly, without stopping, jerking, or reversing.

It is easier to keep going at a high speed. When this is achieved, gradually slow down until you have found the slowest possible treadling rate. When you begin to spin a slow treadling speed is essential. Having mastered the art of continuous movement of the wheel, practise stopping and starting. Use the foot and ankle so as to exert the least possible effort. Many spinners work without shoes to avoid any restriction of movement in the foot.

If the wheel is in good order, treadling should be easy. If not, try loosening the tension screw a little and check the lubrication of the axle bearings, spindle bearings, the spindle shaft and the pivots on the treadle.

Check the cord between the footman and treadle. It should be tied so that the treadle never drops below the horizontal position.

46. A well designed wheel for both beginner and expert

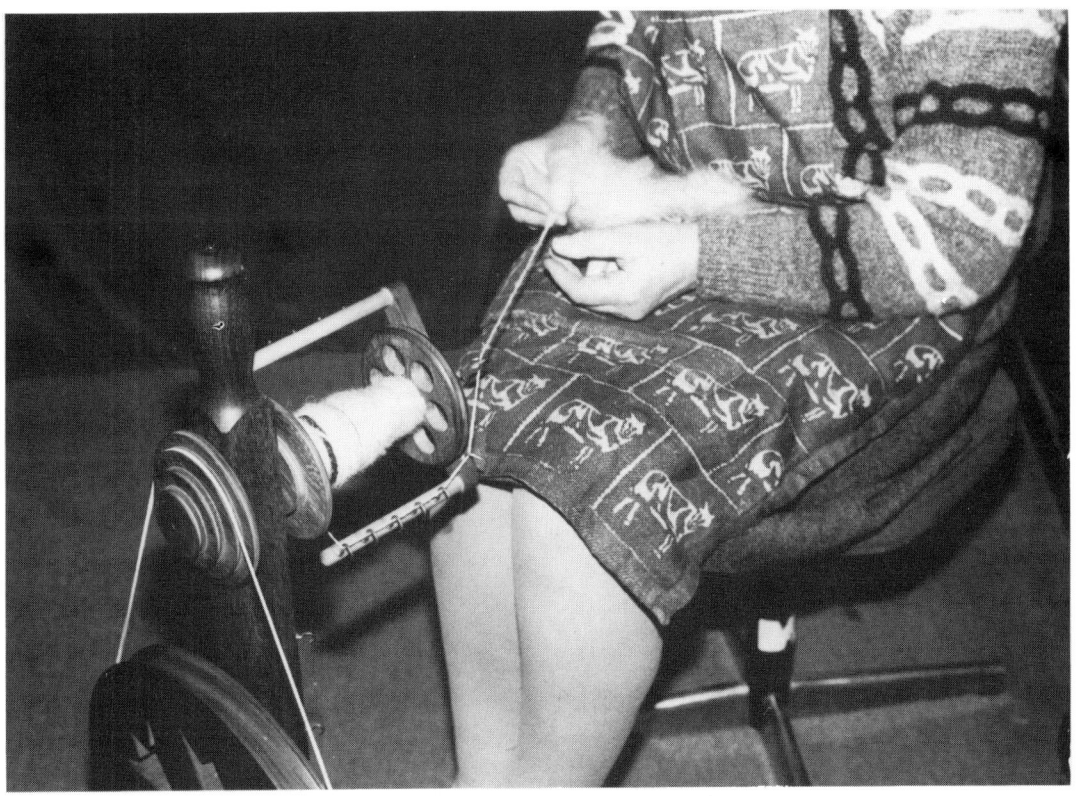

47. Close up of wheel on page 48

A wheel which has been unused for some time may be clogged with grease and dirt, making treadling heavy going. Cleaning off the dirt will make a considerable improvement.

If you are working alone, as a beginner, the easiest way of getting to know the wheel is to practise plying two colours of machine spun yarn.

Tie a length of yarn (a yard or more) on to the bobbin, and lead it over the hooks and through the orifice. If a threading hook has not been supplied with the wheel use a bent hairpin or wire, and keep it where it can be picked up easily — tied by a length of cord to one of the maidens for instance.

Tie the two yarns onto the "leader" and start the wheel turning clockwise. Treadle slowly, helping the knot through the orifice and over the hooks onto the bobbin. With the balls of wool beside you in deep jars, or buckets, let the 2 yarns pass through the fingers on to the bobbins as you treadle.

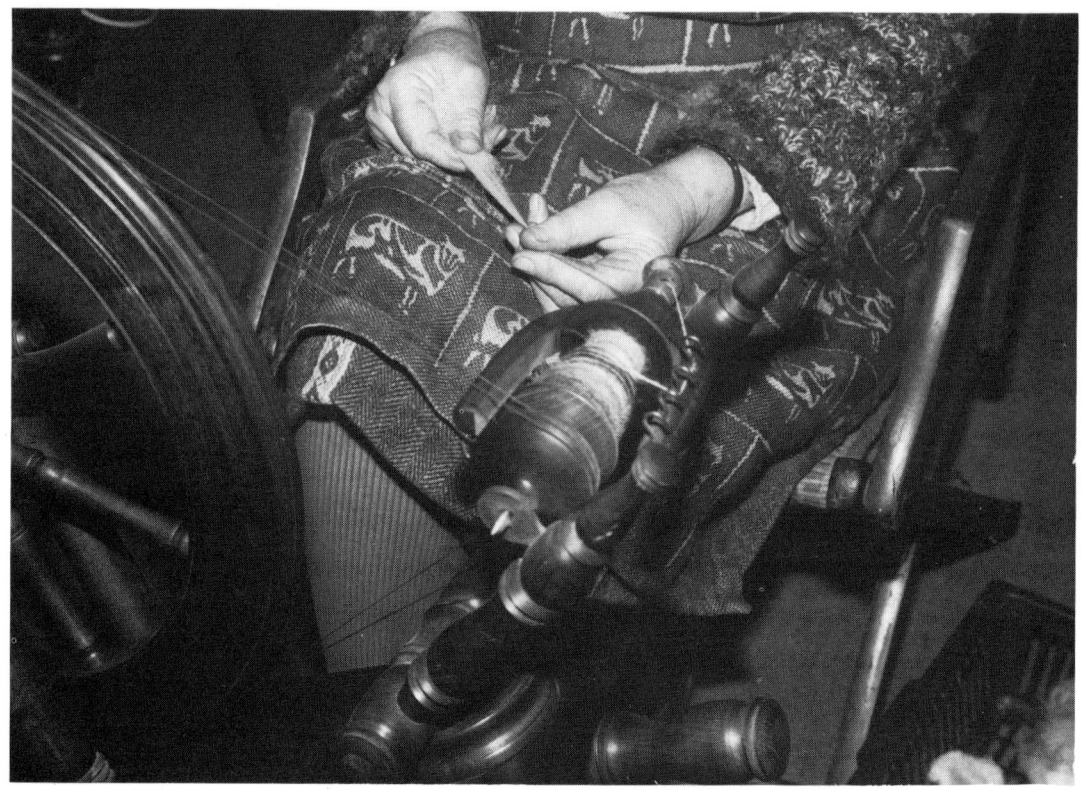

48. *Close up of flyer on double band wheel*

After a time stop and look at the amount of twist on the plied yarn. Alter the tension screw a little, treadle again, and see how it affects the yarn produced.

If you have a choice of pulley size, see what difference that makes to the rate of winding on to the bobbin and the amount of twist.

The working of the wheel is easier to understand after these experiments, and spinning can be attempted with greater confidence.

Remove the plied yarn before starting to spin, but leave the "leader" on the wheel.

Notice which way the yarn winds on to the bobbin, so that you can more easily find a lost end when the yarn breaks and runs on to the bobbin.

Spinning on the Wheel

When you feel ready to spin on the wheel, make sure you have chosen a chair of the right height so that you can treadle easily, and the hands can work comfortably at the height of the orifice. The distance from wheel to chair will vary according to the type of treadle. The wheel may tend to slide away from you on a polished floor. If so, use some sort of non-slip floor covering.

Start with the leader, (which has been tied to the bobbin and led over the hooks and through the eye), held between the first finger and thumb of the left hand, from underneath the yarn.

Hold the prepared fleece in the right hand, with a few strands drawn out.

Start the wheel, and when most of the leader has been drawn in overlap the end with the drawn out fibres and give a sharp twist with finger and thumb. When you feel that the new threads have caught on to the leader, begin to spin from the fleece.

Work with the left hand under the yarn, holding with finger and thumb a few inches from the orifice, while the right hand holds the fleece. (Ill. 49)

The first finger and thumb of the right hand should open and close to control the release of fibres, while the left hand draws gently on the threads, and, inch by inch at first, releases spun yarn to wind on to the bobbin.

The yarn is drawn out between the hands, and when twisted sufficiently, allowed to slide through on to the bobbin. The left hand alternately pinches while the yarn is drawn out and relaxes as it goes on to the bobbin. The right hand alternately releases fibres to take the spin, and grips the main fibre supply to prevent the spin running too far back. (Ill. 50)

Treadle as slowly as possible, but keep going. If the wheel stops and reverses the yarn may break, or jump off the hooks on the flyer.

If the yarn seems to be pulling itself out of your hands and on to the bobbin, slacken the tension a little — not too much, or the thread will not wind on to the bobbin at all.

There is a tendency to overspin at first, making kinks in the yarn which catch in the hooks, preventing the thread from winding on. When this happens, help the yarn on to the bobbin so that it will draw in when spinning is continued.

Your first yarn will probably be uneven, with unspun "slubs" and overspun spirals, and there will be frequent breaks. Try to work at a distance from the eye, so that the broken end is less likely to disappear on to the bobbin. Finding the end can be time-consuming! A wheel with a movable eye on the flyer instead of the usual hooks makes it much easier to find the end — it should be just under the eye.

Move the yarn along the hooks on the flyer regularly, (each time you pick up more fleece) to distribute the yarn evenly, and try to remember which hook you are using so that you know where to look for the broken end.

To join on a new rolag, or prepared fleece, overlap a few fibres on to the spun end, and continue as before. A broken end may be very tightly spun. If so, untwist the last few inches to make it easier to join the new fibres on to the end.

If the fleece is not drawing out easily, your combing, teasing, or carding may be at fault. Without using the wheel, try drafting out some of the prepared fleece and see how well it draws out into a long sliver.

Wool prepared for spinning, then stored for some time, can be made easier to handle if it is put in a warm place for a few hours, to loosen the grease.

Gritty or sandy fleece does not draw out smoothly. It can be spun, but washing would result in a better yarn. Experience will show how to judge whether a fleece is "clean" for spinning in the grease.

Your yarn may be strong and fairly even, except for slubs, the result of pinching unspun fibres with the front hand, then spinning beyond that point. Pinch **spun** yarn, so that all the unspun fibres can be drawn out.

As the present generation has a much higher proportion of left handers individual spinners can decide which way they prefer to work. With an upright wheel it is as easy to work left handed as right handed. With a large horizontal wheel the traditional right handed method may be easier.

FACING PAGE

49. Left hand grips spun yard, right hand draws out fibres

50. Left hand relaxes as spun yarn goes into the bobbin

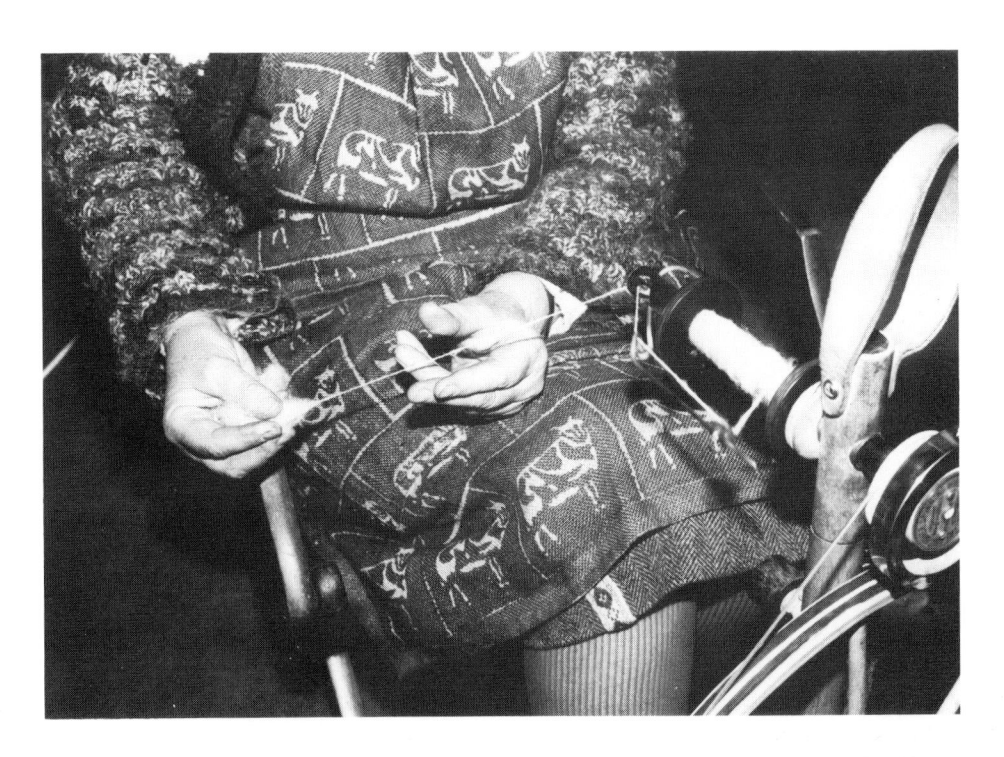

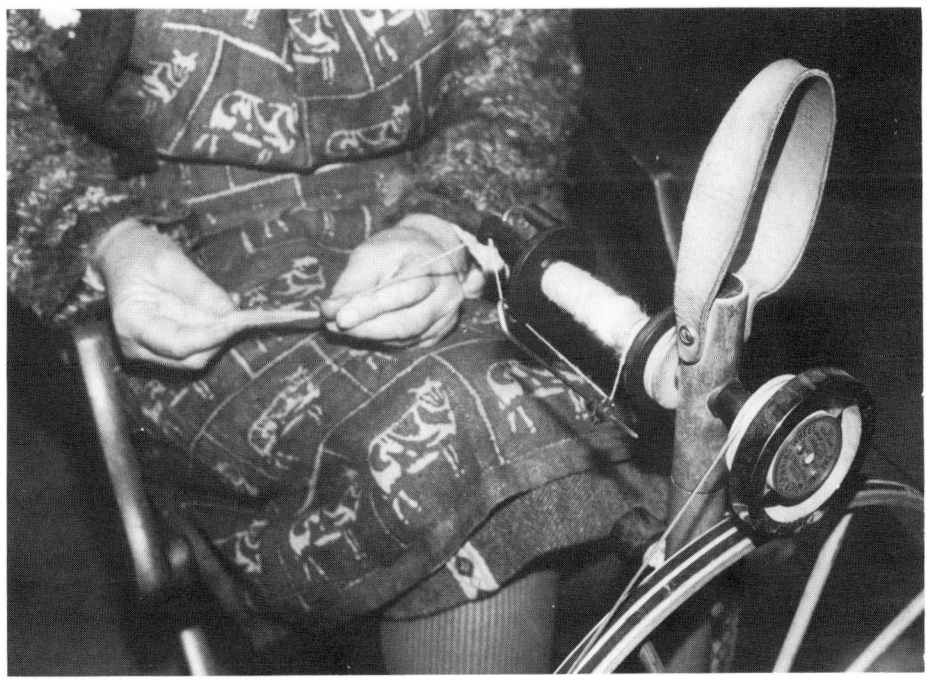

51. *Wheel with large orifice and bobbin for bulky yarn*

52. *Yarns spun by 'short draw' method*

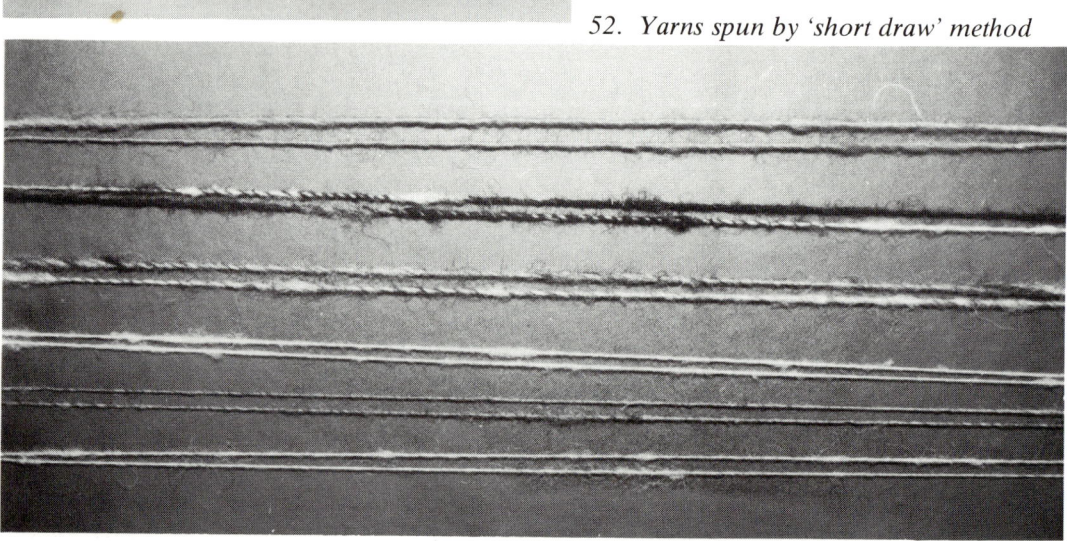

Improving your spinning

To make the most of different wools, showing their characteristics to the best advantage, it is useful to have a working knowledge of a variety of spinning techniques.

The method described so far is the "short draw". The traditional method for rapid wool spinning of short stapled fibres is the "long draw", and worsted spinning, making a smooth yarn from longer fibres is a special "short draw". There are various adaptations which combine elements of these methods, to make a yarn suited to the fibres being spun, and the use of the finished yarn.

Long Draw

To make the traditional woollen yarn, well carded fleece is essential, so that a soft airy yarn can be spun at speed.

Short fibred fleece, carded into rolags so that the fibres are arranged in a spiral, will produce a true woollen yarn. A wheel with a high drive ratio should be used for wool spinning, or when a high spinning rate is achieved the treadling foot will be overworked.

Start with the hands near together, a few inches from the orifice, the left hand holding fibres drawn from the rolag over the end of the leader, right hand lightly holding the rolag.

Treadle to join into the leader, as before, then begin the long draw.

The left hand stays in the same position, near the orifice, all the time, sometimes pinching the yarn, sometimes relaxing.

Close left finger and thumb on yarn, and treadle to build up spin between hand and wheel. (Ill. 53)

Release the grip with the left hand, to let spin run up into the prepared fibres, and AT THE SAME TIME draw back with the right hand, controlling the amount of released fibre with finger and thumb.

The left hand alternately opens and closes to control the twist running up, and the right hand continues to draw back. (Ill. 54)

There is a definite pull on the lengthening yarn, partly from the wheel, partly from the left hand.

When the yarn has been drawn out to the full stretch of the right arm, the left hand relaxes and the yarn is allowed to wind on to the bobbin, until once again the hands are a few inches apart and a grip is taken with the left hand to build up the twist.

53. *Treadle to build spin*

54. *Draw out to the full length of the arm*

56

55. Traditional wheel for long draw spinning

56. Modern wheel equally good for long draw method

The number of beats on the treadle will vary from wheel to wheel, but when the right amount of twist has been established a rhythmic sequence can be repeated.

a) Both hands near orifice, count 1, 2, 3, 4, to accumulate twist.

b) Release spin, drawing out rolag with right hand, controlling release of twist with left hand, counting reaching twelve when arm is at full stretch.

c) Yarn winding on, held by right hand only, count reaching fifteen as hands come together again and left hand grips again to accumulate twist.

When taking a new rolag, move the yarn on to the next hook on the flyer, so that the thread is distributed evenly along the bobbin. On a double drive hand wheel, after leading the thread along all the hooks and back again, tighten the tension screw very slightly.

It will take time to perfect these movements, but when they are mastered, airy wool can be produced at speed.

Worsted and Half Worsted Spinning – Preparation.

To spin a true worsted yarn the fleece must be combed so that all the short fibres are removed. For most handspinners a "half worsted" is a satisfactory compromise, and it is particularly suitable for plying as a knitting yarn. Lustrous wools show off to great advantage when spun this way, as the parallel arrangement of fibres reflects the light, giving the yarn a silky sheen.

Few longwool fleeces are ideal for woollen spinning. They do not "bulk up" during the finishing process, and their long staple makes them unsuitable for preparation on hand carders. They are better spun as worsted or half worsted.

The fleece should be prepared for spinning by opening up locks of wool, either with the fingers or with a comb, keeping the fibres parallel and letting grit and seeds drop out. The fibres must be free, so that they can be drawn out smoothly.

Drum carded wool is suitable, so long as the batts are not too thick. The fibre must be thoroughly combed. Strips should be torn off the batt for spinning.

Often the best fleece for half worsted spinning (a good Romney, for instance) is so "open" and clean the preparation is very quick and compensates for the slower spinning rate compared with wool spinning.

Keep the prepared wool with the ends pointing the same way, and placed so that they can be picked up easily for spinning.

57. Beautifully finished wheel ideal for worsted type spinning

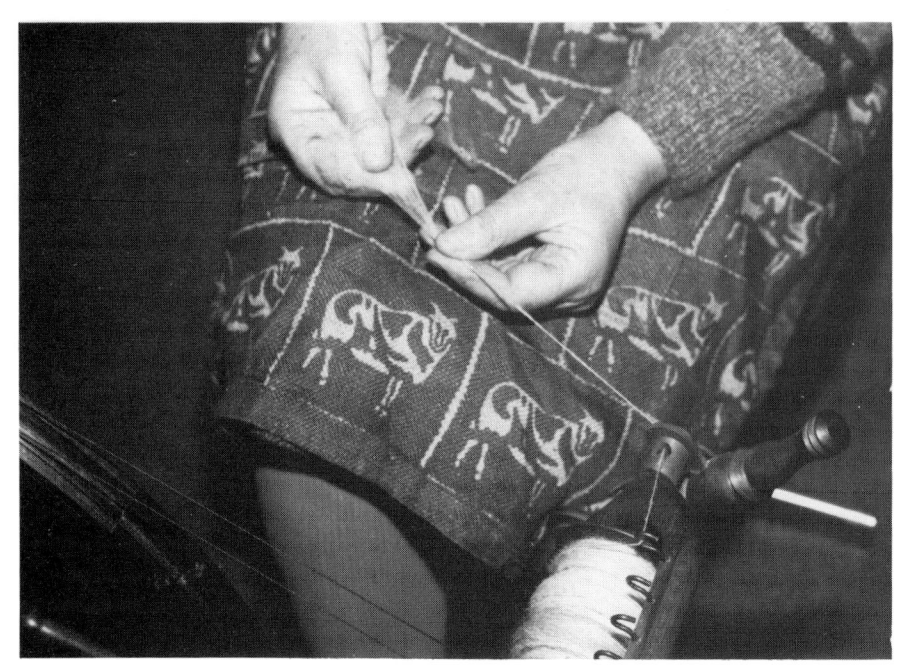

58. *Drawing fibres from the fleece*

59. *Left hand smooths yarn as it's drawn in*

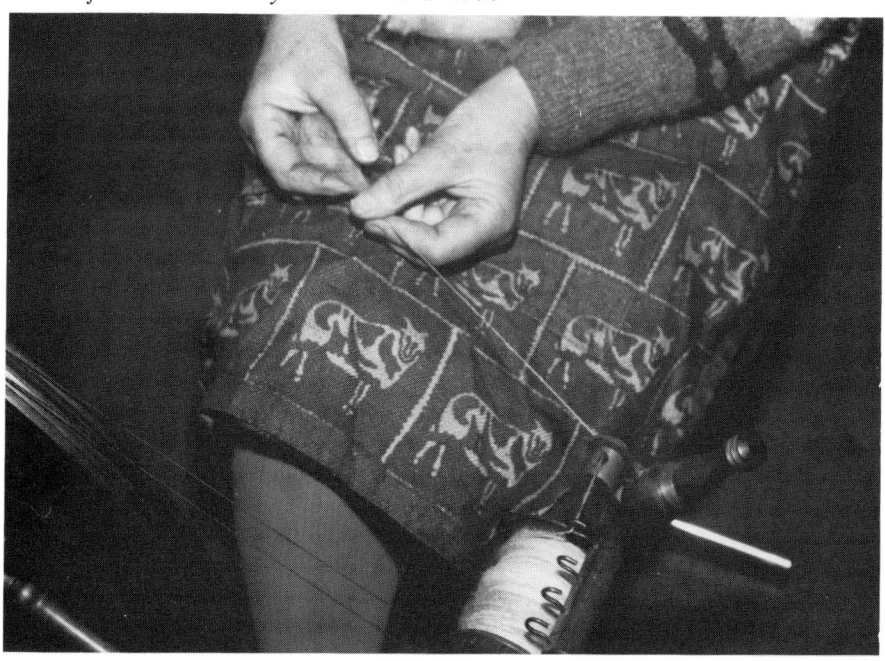

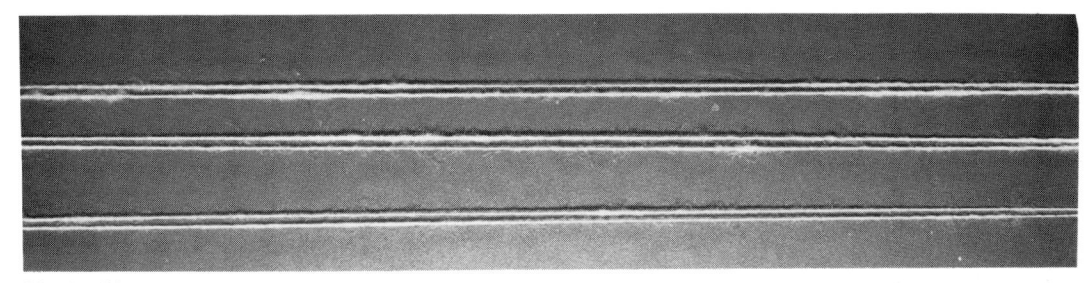

60. Half worsted yarns

Spinning

Take a little of the prepared wool, draw out a few fibres to join in the usual way.

Treadle slowly, and start to spin, drawing fibres from the fleece so that they make a fan shape between finger and thumb of the hand holding the wool supply. (Ill. 58)

The front hand moves up and down, drawing off fibres and smoothing the yarn, and the other hand stays in the same position, holding the fibre supply. (Ill. 59)

The tension comes from the hand holding the fleece and the gentle pull of the wheel, the yarn being gradually drawn in as you work.

Experience will show the amount of twist suitable to the character of the fleece, and as in all spinning, a steady rhythm is needed to produce a yarn of constant thickness and quality. (Ill. 60)

Remember that if the yarn is going to be plied, the amount of twist will be reduced in the finished yarn.

Too much twist will make a hard, over-spun yarn, which will not show off the good qualities of the fleece. Too little twist produces a weak thread. The character of the yarn depends on the fineness and softness of the fibres and the length of the staple. Obviously long stapled fibres can be drawn out to a fine thread without breaking, but often a fine hand-spun needs to be soft, too. The harder long wools make strong warp yarn for furnishing fabrics or hardwearing tweeds. Worsted type yarns make a "cooler" cloth than the air-filled woollen yarns.

Medium Draw

The method described for learning to spin is the "short draw", and the traditional woollen spin is the "long draw". A usefull adaptation comes between the two, so it could be called the "medium draw".

The spin is controlled by the front hand, and the rear hand draws back just beyond the twist, until about half a yard of yarn is ready to wind on. The front hand helps to smooth in stray fibres as the yarn goes on its way to the bobbin. As so much spun thread is visible, it is easy to judge when to add a little more twist, or draw out a little more, to achieve the required yarn.

As control improves, treadling rate can be increased, and yarn produced at a reasonable speed.

Spinning soft Yarns

When spinning soft, fine wools, great care must be taken so that the fibres are not stretched. These wools must be treated gently at every stage — washing, rinsing, drying, teasing, carding, spinning and plying.

Usually fine soft fleece is spun into fine yarn, but if a soft bulky yarn is required, increase the tension on the wheel and treadle more slowly than usual, as with fine wool there are many more fibres to control.

The soft feel of the finished wool comes partly from the quality of the fleece, and partly from the spinning.

Gradually the fingers become more sensitive to the "feel" of the fleece, and if the preparation has been thorough it is possible to spin a soft yarn with very little help from the left hand. The wheel tension is adjusted so that it draws in very gently, and the rolag is held lightly in the right hand. (Ill. 61) Treadle fairly quickly, and as the right hand draws back against the slight pull of the wheel, the yarn can be wound on almost continuously to produce a thread with just enough twist for a soft yarn. A little practice is needed to get it right, but once mastered it is a quick and easy way to spin a soft thread.

Spinning Fine Yarns

Fine yarns can be spun by any of the methods described. The secret is to start with well prepared fleece — well carded, well combed, or simply well prepared in the hand.

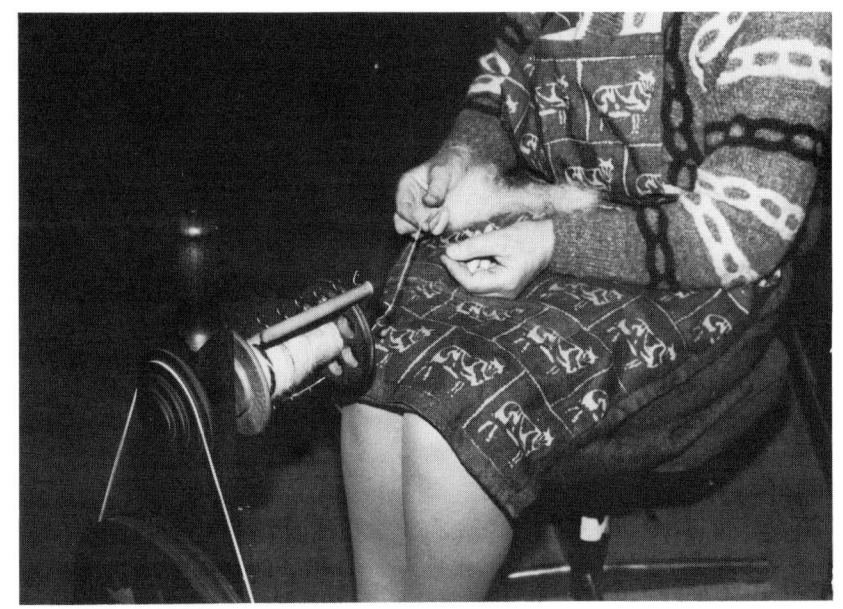

61. Fleece held lightly in right hand

Use only the best fleece — it is a waste of time to spin a fine yarn if it looks like sewing thread. The "down" breeds, Southdown in particular, Merino crosses, fine Romney, Shetland and Gotland, for instance, are well worth the effort of spinning fine.

Nimble fingers are essential to spin a fine yarn from short fibres, but it can be done, and the result repays the time spent.

If the yarn is to be used single, remember none of the twist will be removed by plying, so put just the amount of spin required in the finished yarn. Singles can be used satisfactorily for crochet work, and, if the amount of twist is judged correctly, for knitting, too.

Let the yarn rest on the bobbin for a few days to "set" before skeining. A very delicate singles from a fleece which is liable to felt to any great extent, (Merino cross, for instance) is probably better left unwashed until the garment is finished, as it can so easily be spoiled by washing the skein.

Shetland and Gotland (a fine lustrous fleece of delicate pearly shades, well worth searching out) can be spun fine without the worries of over-felting and shrinking. The stole in Ill. 62 is 2′ × 6′ and weighs less than 2oz, including the thick fringe. The wool is still soft and "warm" when spun to 400yds per ounce, and could be drawn out finer.

62. Lightweight stole made of fine spun wool

Plying and Finishing

If you intend to knit your handspun yarn, it should be plied to give strength and make a more uniform yarn. Stitches of knitted singles tend to twist. Plied yarn keeps its shape.

You will have noticed that your handspun, when doubled, tends to twist into a 2 ply yarn.

When two singles are plied, they are twisted in the opposite direction from the original spin. If the singles were spun clockwise —Z twist — they will be plied anti clockwise — S twist. Although usually two strands only are plied, at a later stage you may try 3 or 4 ply.

The thickness of the yarn obviously depends on the thickness of the original singles and a 2 ply may be cobweb fine or as thick as your thumb.

Some wheels have built-in bobbin stands, but they are not always suitably placed for plying. Some "Lazy Kates" sold for the purpose, are inefficient, too, as they are top-heavy or the movement of the bobbin loosens the axle-pin, letting the bobbin drop out.

A solidly built bobbin stand which stays firmly in place is a great help. However, a cheap improvisation can be made quickly with a boot box and a few skewers or knitting needles. The bobbins must revolve freely so that plying can proceed smoothly. (Ill. 63)

Old wheels rarely have spare bobbins, so the yarn must be fed to the wheel by some other method. Roughly wound balls of wool are not ideal, but if you have a ball winder, so that the yarn can be drawn from the centre, plying is more successful. The balls can be placed in buckets, to prevent them rolling around the floor.

If you are a weaver, and have the use of a spool winder, singles can be plied from spools placed on a rack.

Bobbins or spools should start equally loaded.

Place your bobbin rack beside you, sit at your wheel and tie the two ends of yarn on to the leader.

Let the two singles run separately on each side of the middle finger of one hand, and keep that hand close to the body, opposite the orifice.

With just enough tension to draw in, start to treadle, with the wheel turning anti clockwise (the reverse direction from that used to spin the singles).

Help the knot through the orifice, over the hooks and on to the bobbin.

Keep the hand holding the singles close to the body so that the yarn in the twisting zone is kept taut, treadle to build up the spin (4 or 5 times, for instance), then pinch the plied yarn with the fingers of the front hand and help it forward quickly on to the bobbin, thus bringing more singles to be plied. (Ill. 64)

Repeat the rhythm of a number of treadle beats, and a quick wind-on, then look at the plied yarn and decide whether it would be improved with more twist or with less. If the yarn looks too hard, reduce the number of treadles. If it looks sloppy, add one beat.

An alternative method of plying is to let the pull from the wheel draw in the plied yarn at a constant rate, without pausing to build up spin before allowing the yarn to wind on.

Simply let the singles run separately through the fingers and forward to the orifice, treadling at the rate which produces the right amount of twist.

Try both methods, and decide which is more successful.

As the appearance and feel of the yarn can be so different after washing, it may take a number of experiments to make the plied yarn you hoped for, so make a note of what you are doing, so that you can repeat it later.

Joins can spoil the rhythm of plying, varying the amount of twist near the join, so, at first, make a knot if a join has to be made. Mark it with a piece of contrasting yarn, so that later on the knots can be easily found and taken out.

As you put twist into the plied yarn, you take it out of the singles. Seeing the effect of plying will help to plan the amount of twist on singles in future.

When the yarn is being plied to your satisfaction, carry on working with a regular rhythm. There should be little worry about chasing broken ends, so sit back and relax. You will probably be able to treadle much more quickly than when spinning singles, but do not forget to move the yarn along to fill the bobbin evenly. As you do not have to stop to pick up fresh fleece, the tendency is to carry on for too long without changing hooks. Aim at an even distribution, so that the bobbin can be filled completely.

As the singles are untwisted through being plied in the reverse direction, the yarn becomes softer and more bulky, so two bobbins loaded with singles will fill more than two bobbins with plied wool.

If the telephone rings while you are plying, do not leap up and leave the yarns loose, or when you return it will be difficult to carry

63. Home made bobbin stand with added tensioning device

on evenly. Twist the yarn from the orifice round some part of the wheel — one of the maidens, perhaps — so that the plied yarn stays as you left it until you can resume work.

64. Plying using home made bobbin stand

Designing your Yarns

As the various techniques of preparing fleece, spinning and plying are mastered, it is possible to spin wool with a particular project in mind — you are designing the yarn.

Plying gives scope for producing a variety of yarns. The twist of the singles can be matched in the plying, or one can be greater than the other.

Two fine yarns, lightly spun and lightly plied, will make a soft knitting yarn.

A soft bubbly yarn results from plying a bulky singles, lightly spun, with a fine firmly spun thread.

Plying in the same direction as the original spin makes the yarn firmer, and in the opposite direction makes it softer, so by plying singles which were spun in opposite directions, interesting yarns can be made.

Four singles plied together make a softer yarn than that made by two-ply yarns plied together.

By holding the yarns separately in each hand, one can be fed in more quickly than the other, or held back so that the other yarn is wrapped or looped around it.

By using prepared wool of two colours, you can add to the variety. Prepare the colours separately, and, holding them together in the hand, make a two-colour yarn. By careful manipulation many different effects can be produced.

If equal amounts are drawn from the two rolags, and spun together, the yarn looks rather like a 2-ply. Fibres drawn from each colour in turn gives quite à different effect.

The result of spinning a Jacob fleece completely at random can be very disappointing with yards of dark followed by yards of light, but when well managed the colour variations can be very attractive indeed.

To make a range of shades from dark to light, vary the proportions of the two colours — one part dark to one, three or five of light, for instance — when the fleece is prepared for spinning. To make an even blend for each shade, card carefully, twice if necessary. Alternatively tease the fleece well and toss together in a heap on the floor, turning it until the colours are mixed, then card it.

Make further ranges of shades by plying singles from different blends.

Yarn plied from different colours of yarn, either sharply contrasting or just varying in shade, makes a "tweedy" effect.

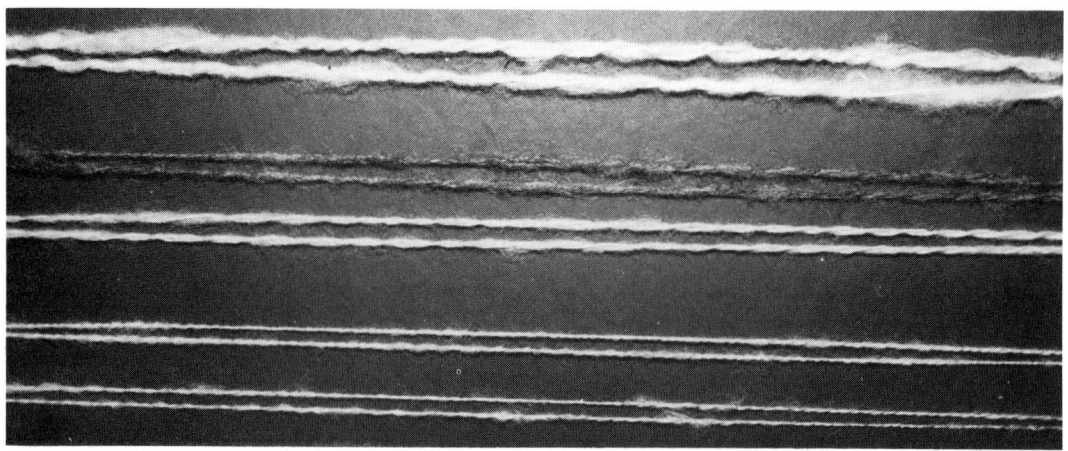

65. A variety of plied yarns

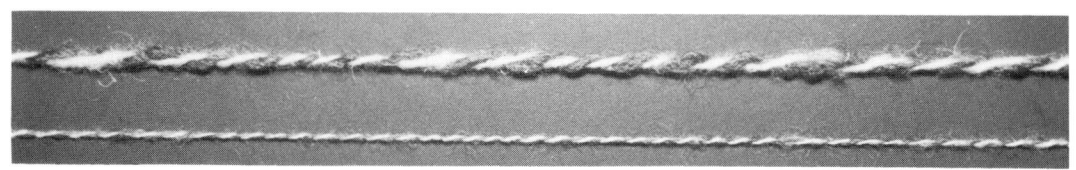

66. Contrasting 2 colour plied yarns

For a flecked yarn, add small pieces, from combings too short to spin alone, to prepared fleece of another colour. They will be more firmly spun into the yarn if added when carding, but the coloured spots are more obvious if they are incorporated during spinning.

For a firm, hard textured yarn, the singles can be "cabled", by plying with the wheel turning in the same direction as the singles were originally spun. In this case, care must be taken not to overspin the original singles.

A 4 ply crepe yarn can be spun by plying two two-ply yarns in the same direction as the original twist — Z singles, S plied, then this yarn Z plied. This makes a springy yarn which is very good for knitted garments as it keeps its shape.

Experiment to find how to produce the yarn you want. Plying gives great scope for designing yarns, and some of the accidental effects may be worth repeating deliberately.

Keep a note of your methods of spinning and plying, with a sample of the original fleece, so that you gradually make your own reference book. As different fleeces, even from the same breed, can vary considerably, results will vary, too.

Skeining the Yarn

"If the yarn is going to be plied, this should be done before skeining and washing it. Wool plied after it has been washed looks like two yarns twisted together rather than a "whole" yarn.

A skein winder of some kind — a niddy noddy or a swift — is a good investment, so that hanks can be made of uniform size. By measuring the circumference and counting the threads, the length of yarn can be calculated.

Yarn intended for weaving, particularly for the warp, should have no knots in the skeins. If there is a break, start a new skein, so that when making the warp no knots will appear in inconvenient places.

Before skeining, singles yarns should be left on the bobbin for a few days to "set" if possible.

Very delicate singles, like Merino or Merino cross should be used straight from the bobbin. Washing can be left until the article (probably a lacy shawl) has been made.

67. Washed skeins drying on niddy noddies

If the yarn is being taken direct from the wheel, slacken the tension when making the skein, so that the bobbin runs freely.

When skeining your plied yarn, stand the completed bobbin several feet from your skein winder. This helps to smooth out any uneven patches in your yarn.

Make sure the ends of the wool are tied so that they can be found easily after washing, and secure the skein with figure-of-eight ties in several places. This is to keep the skein in order, yet to allow the washing liquid to penetrate the entire skein. (Ill. 24) If it has been well spun and plied, the skein should hang straight when held by one of the ties. If the "balance" is wrong it will twist.

The size of the skein should be in proportion to the thickness of the yarn. One or two ounces will be sufficient for fine wool, four ounces for heavier wool. The bobbin may hold twice as much as this, but a very thick hank is difficult to wash evenly, so split a large bobbin load into two or more skeins.

Take a note of the weight and length of your yarn before it is washed, so that it can be compared with length and weight after washing.

Washing your skeins

As when washing fleece, care must be taken to avoid felting the wool. Soft, fine wools need extra care. There should be no rubbing, twisting or temperature shocks. Do not use a detergent which removes **all** the grease, or you will have a dry, lifeless yarn.

Wet wool will overstretch unless its weight is supported, so lift skeins carefully to avoid over-stretching.

Never leave the wool under a running tap. Have the bowl of warm suds ready, and put in the skeins with as little movement of the water as possible.

Do not rush. It takes quite a time for the wool to get thoroughly wet, so leave it to soak.

Squeeze out surplus water gently. Rinse thoroughly in several changes of warm water.

Squeeze out when clean, still avoiding any twisting. Roll in a towel to absorb surplus water, or, with skeins in an old pillow case, use a spin drier or wringer, but not a tumble drier.

Dry the wool out of doors if possible, but not in strong sunlight, which could make the yarn yellow. Worsted yarn, and any yarn inclined to "kink" should be weighted slightly as it dries, but take care not to overstretch the wool. The skeins can be hung on a rod, with a second, weighted rod at the bottom, or the skeins can be hung individually with separate weights.

Before hanging to dry, shake the skeins to free the strands, and shake them again when they are dry.

Measure the washed skein, and weigh it. If the wool was spun "in the grease" there may be a considerable loss of weight, as well as a noticeable shrinkage. This can be as much as six inches in the yard in a Southdown or Merino yarn, but very little in the longwools. Loss of weight varies considerably, too. It can easily be one third the original weight from a gritty, greasy wool, but very little from a clean, well sorted fleece.

Until you know from experience what to expect, assume that your yarn will be only half the weight of the original fleece.

Occasionally skeins of wool spun in the grease are difficult to wash because they have been left for a long time and the grease has hardened. Place the skeins in a pan of cold water. Bring slowly to simmering point, then move away from the heat. When rinsed, the wool should have softened.

68. Skeins of plied yarns after washing

70. *Old Scottish click reel*

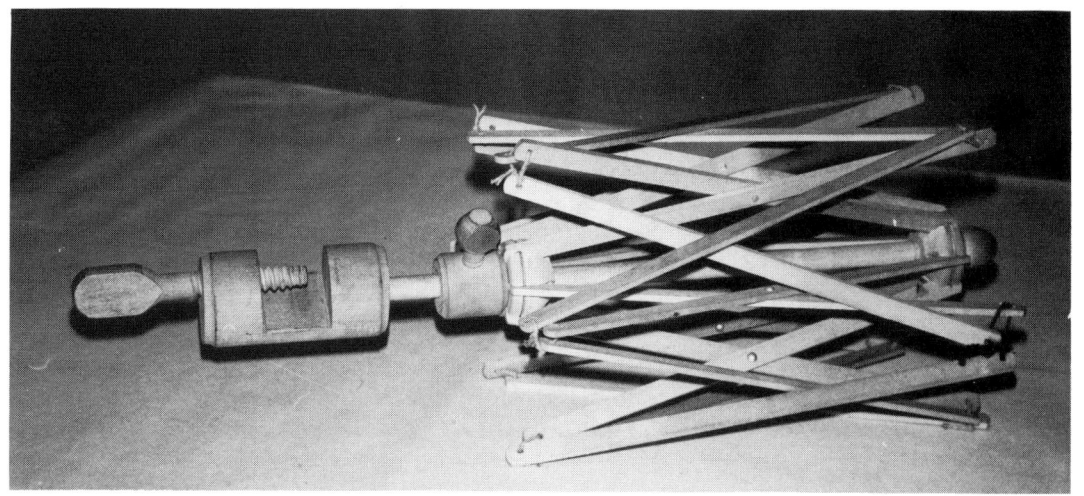

69. Folding swift

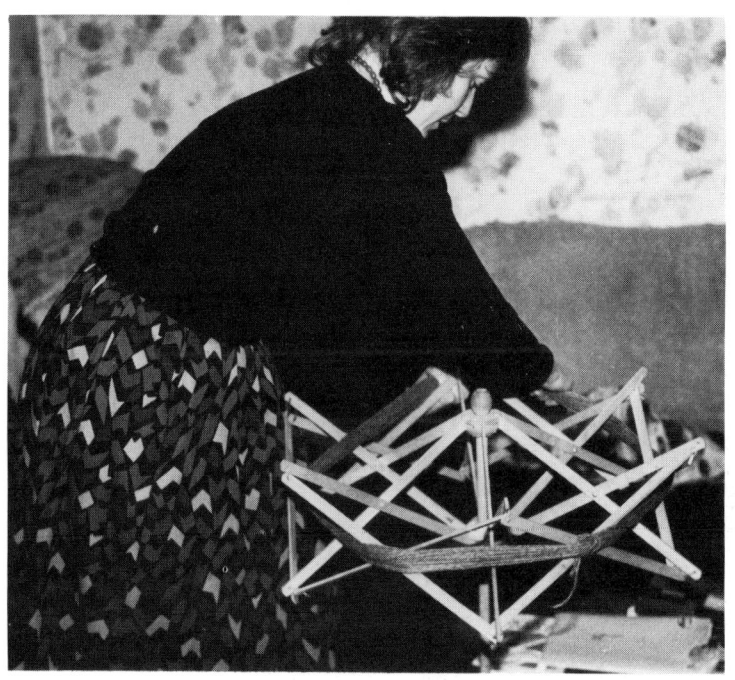

71. Winding washed wool from the swift

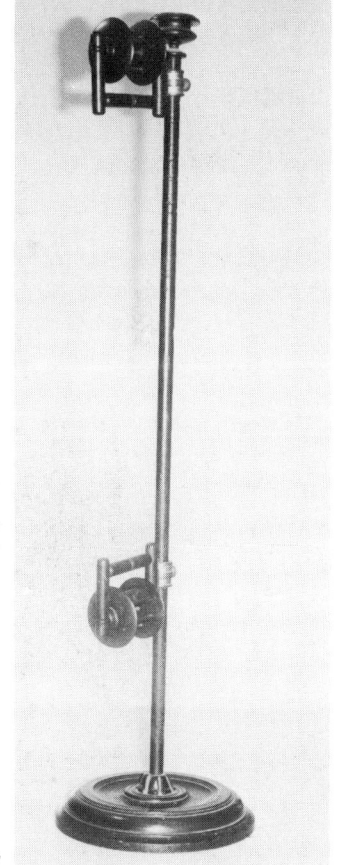

72. Old swift for winding yarns into balls

Other animal fibres

Many animal fibres can be spun into satisfactory yarns. You can buy prepared mohair, camel hair, etc from suppliers in the conventional way, or you can go direct to the source of supply. Next time you visit a wild life park, or a zoo, look at the coats of the animals there. If you like the thought of spinning them ask if you can buy what you need. For something really special there may be a waiting list, but you may hear of some other keeper of exotic animals who could supply you.

When using camel hair, separate the coarse outer coat from the fine underlayer. The long outer hair is easily combed for spinning. The soft undercoat should be teased and carded. It can be blended with wool or spun alone. In the latter case it will need more twist than wool.

Llama hair can be treated in the same way as wool of similar length.

Your fibre supplier may be the family pet.

Hair from some breeds of dog is quite easy to spin from a handful of combings, without any preparation. Often dog hair is blended with fleece "in the grease". Dog hair doesn't "hold" as well as wool, so when spinning use a short draw. Yarn spun from the hair of our liver-and-white English Springer Spaniel looks rather like mohair, and is best spun to a fairly bulky yarn.

Handling the fur of Angora rabbit is easier if the hands are sprinkled with talcum powder.

There is something particularly satisfying in knowing exactly which animal provides the raw materials for a spun yarn.

73. Camel hair-soft undercoat on left, outer hair on right

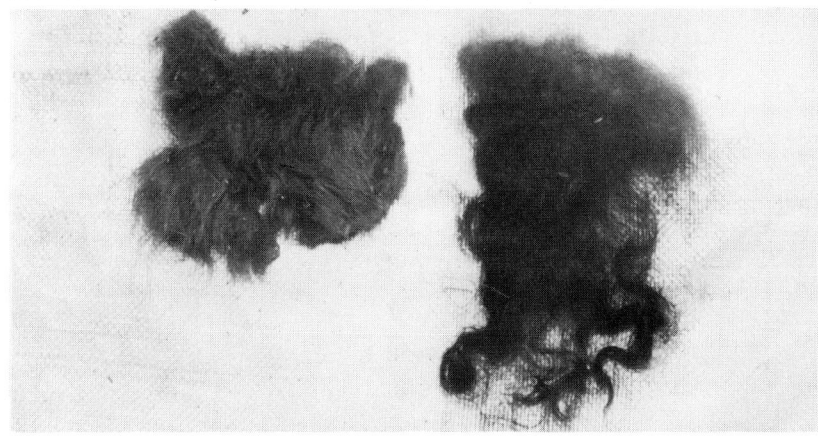

Using Your Handspun

Weaving

Handspun yarn can be used for weaving, knitting, crochet, embroidery, or any other craft using threads. Rough spun yarns are probably best used in weaving, where the uneven texture makes lively wall hangings and rugs.

Scarves, stoles, knee rugs and cot blankets have a "cosy" look when made with a beginner's yarn. The warp should not be too closely packed or the weft beaten too hard; see that the characteristic "chunky" weave is well displayed. Make the most of your first yarns. It is very difficult to imitate the style later!

As the texture of the beginner's yarn is its own decoration, a plain weave is all that is required. Weave a folded cloth on a four shaft loom to make a wider rug, but make sure that the warp yarn can take the necessary tension. If a few threads stretch it can be difficult weaving a double cloth.

A soft bulky yarn with sufficient strength for the purpose is shown off well in a hopsack weave, spaced to show the character of the yarn.

A yarn required for warp must be strong enough to withstand a certain amount of tension, as well as the friction from the reed and heddle eyes, so in sorting wool for warp and weft, bear this in mind. Just a few inches of weak, underspun yarn can mean a stretched or broken warp thread, needing time-consuming repairs. If your handspun yarn is not strong enough for a warp, use machine spun yarn instead.

It is possible to buy wool spun for handweavers to match your own handspun yarn, and this can be used in combination with your own wool.

If you have a simple frame loom, use it with a strong warp to make firm weft faced fabrics for bags, chair seats and hangings.

Harsher handspun yarns are ideal for weaving floor rugs and furnishing fabrics, and the natural colours of these yarns give great scope for individuality.

Even a two-shaft loom can be used to make interesting patterns, and with a four-shaft loom a simple threading like rosepath produces a variety of borders or repeat patterns. A number of articles can be made on one warp, using oddments of handspun with other yarns.

A few throws of a soft bulky thread in a cloth woven mainly of finer yarn makes an interesting effect, or try making a "stripe" in the warp with a thicker yarn. Simple ideas are often the most effective.

Roughspun yarn makes interesting free weaving patterns on improvised frames of metal or wood.

Particularly with uneven spinning, woven garments are difficult to plan because cut edges present a problem. Try combining weaving with knitting or crochet. Using weaving for the back and front, add knitted sleeves. Make the fronts of a waistcoat on a loom, and crochet the back and buttonhole bands.

An expert is not limited in choosing a project for weaving, but beginners hesitate to use their first efforts.

If each skein is labelled with its weight and length it should be easy to work out how much yarn is required for a particular project.

Remember when calculating the length of the warp to allow for wastage, which varies according to the loom being used. If the knots at the beginning of the weaving are carefully unpicked the ends can be used as a fringe, so that there is no waste of your carefully spun wool.

Decide on the number and length of warp ends to work out the amount required for the warp.

Similarly, from the width, and the number of throws per inch, the length of weft yarn can be calculated.

Always prepare much more yarn than you expect ot use.

Finishing your weaving — washing and tentering — completes the picture. As in all stages of the work, rougher yarns stand up to rougher treatment, but fine soft handspun needs to be handled with care, as it is more liable to felting and shrinking than tougher wools.

Wash gently, and rinse well. Dry on a tenter frame if possible, or place on softboard and use pins round the edge of the weaving to keep it in shape. Leave undisturbed to dry.

Handspun yarn is suitable for finger weaving, but for inkle or tablet weaving it is advisable to wait until you can make a smooth yarn. A closely packed warp has to stand up to constant friction during the weaving process, so a firm plied worsted type yarn is needed.

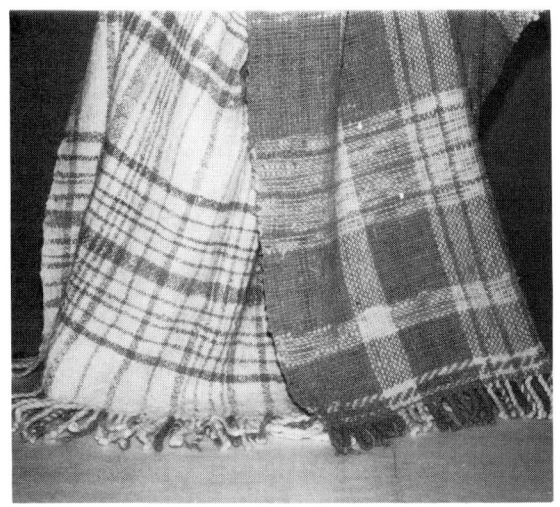

74. Rugs woven from beginner's yarn

75. Bags and stole woven from beginner's yarn

76. Close up of stole

Knitting

More and more knitters, tired of man-made fibres, decide to spin their own wool. It is very satisfying to make a garment of yarn of exactly the colour, thickness and texture you want, instead of using whatever happens to be on sale at the time.

A knitted jersey which is going to survive years of wear should be made of evenly spun, well plied wool, but attractive garments can be made from less skilfully spun yarns, particularly if they have the added interest of natural colour.

Probably your first handspun wool will be somewhat overspun. If it is wound into balls, then knitted with two threads together, the yarns will twist together somewhat as you knit. With luck the thin parts of one thread are worked along with the thicker parts of the other, but this is not an infallible rule! Given a little help, by breaking a thin strand and overlapping it, or adding an extra length of yarn for a short distance, you can achieve quite acceptable results with rough spun wool.

As the quality of your spinning changes quickly, the amount of very uneven yarn may be quite small, and could be used for a cap or mittens. Fairly well spun wool is needed for gloves, or it is difficult to make the fingers of the required size.

Wait until there is enough wool to complete the project planned, and examine the hanks of yarn to compare the quality. They should be labelled with their length and weight. When you wind the wool into balls, tie on the labels again so that you get some idea of the amount you are using.

Before deciding finally on the size of needle and the pattern, knit small squares and see how they look. Your samples are worth saving to make an interesting scrap book of your progress.

When you have found the right size of needle to suit the thickness of the wool, measure the sample square, and count the number of stitches and rows to the inch.

If a firmer yarn is needed for the ribbing of your first handspun garment, knit that part with machine spun wool from the same breed. Jacob knitting wool is readily available, and other kinds — Herdwick, Swaledale and Welsh Mountain wool, for instance — are on the market.

Choose a very simple pattern for your first hand spun garment. A broad rib (knit 6 purl 2, for instance) holds its shape well, and the

*77. Mittens from beginners first wheel spinning. Gloves from first
spindle spinning*

pattern makes it easy to match shapings. Make sure the pattern is
equally balanced across the garment.

As your spinning improves, planning garments becomes easier.
It may be possible to follow a pattern for commercially produced
knitting yarn, if your tension is right both in width and length, but it
takes experience to work out quantities.

Usually plied handspun is lighter in weight than its bulk would
suggest, and it makes a lighter garment than that quoted in the
pattern. However, as commercial yarns vary so much, particularly

when they are of man-made fibres, estimating the weight required is not easy. Keep a record of what you use, with samples of wool and pattern details, and learn from experience.

Machine spun wool intended for weaving is easier to deal with, as thickness and yardage are quoted, but many knitting yarns are difficult to compare with handspun. Now there is the added complication of selling knitting yarn in various metric weights of 20gm, 25gm and 50gm. The old method of selling wool in skeins made it easy to calculate the length, but now wool is usually sold in balls.

The following chart might be of help.

Commercially spun knitting yarns.

1oz.		25gm	
2 ply	200–250 yds	2 ply	125–200m
3 ply	125–150 yds	3 ply	100–120m
4 ply	100–125 yds	4 ply	75–100m
Double knit	60– 75 yds	Double knit	50– 60m
Triple knit	about 45 yds	Triple knit	35m
Chunky	about 30 yds	Chunky	25m

The number of metres in 25gm is equivalent to $4/5$ of the yds per oz.

Yards per oz is $1\frac{1}{4} \times$ metres per 25gm.

Plied handspun generally referred to as "fine" is 150 yards per ounce or more, equivalent to 2- or 3 ply commercial yarns.

"Medium" handspun is about the thickness of 4 ply to double knit.

"Heavy" handspun is thicker than double knitting.

Try the effect of different stitches and needle sizes. If too loosely knitted the garment will not wear well; if too tightly worked, your handspun will not be shown off at its best.

Stocking stitch (one row knit, one row purl) displays any flaws in the spinning. Equally it shows off the good quality of your work.

Ribbing holds its shape, and hides imperfections.

Faults show more clearly in white than in dark colour, and the quality of the spinning is less evident in a yarn of mixed colours. So, if you make a beautiful yarn with a special texture, it will show more clearly if it is a light colour and knitted in stocking stitch; your

78. *6oz dark and jacob wool plied together was used for this simple V neck top*

efforts will be less appreciated if you use dark wool and knit it in ribbing or an ornate pattern.

It is advisable to work from a basic pattern with simple shapes at first, so that it is easy to change the number of stitches to suit the wool.

Most knitting wool manufacturers provide pattern sheets with "family" patterns of garments in a range of sizes. After knitting a sample square, and working out the tension, it should be an easy matter to find how many stitches to cast on, and choose the relevant size from the pattern sheet.

Remember your sample square should be worked in the stitch you intend to use.

Garter stitch (every row knit) makes a fabric wider and shorter than a piece of stocking stitch with the same number of stitches and rows. Garter stitch has a lengthways stretch.

Lacy patterns and cable stitches vary the tension, too, so decide on the pattern before working out the number of stitches to cast on the needle.

Before beginning to knit, and before winding the yarn into balls, examine all the skeins. If they vary, sort them out into different lots. Try to make the main parts of matching wool, and use a different batch for the ribbing, if necessary.

Choose yarn of matching quality for the sleeves. If something different has to be used for part of the back and front, change the stitch, as well as the wool, when you get to the yoke, so that the change of yarn is less obvious, or use a narrow stripe of contrasting wool to separate two batches of wool of the main colour.

If you have to introduce a second colour, make it look planned, not accidental.

By using long needles, and knitting the back and front side by side, it is easy to make them match. Knit the sleeves side by side on one needle, too.

If you are using a familiar pattern which you know will "work", start by knitting the sleeves, when you have all your wool to choose from, because oddments would show up very obviously there. It is reasonably simple to adapt the pattern to work in different yarns in the back and front.

Circular needles are very useful for knitting up to the armholes of a jersey, and, if you wish, you can still use them to work backwards and forwards to the shoulder.

A raglan cardigan, worked up the the armhole shaping using two needles, can be completed on a circular needle, working to and

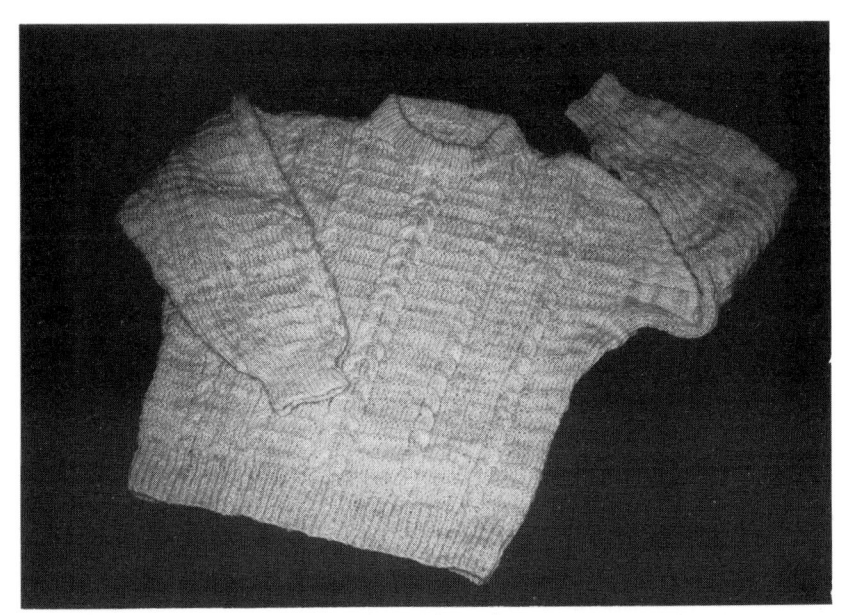

79. Traditional Guernsey pattern with underarm gussets

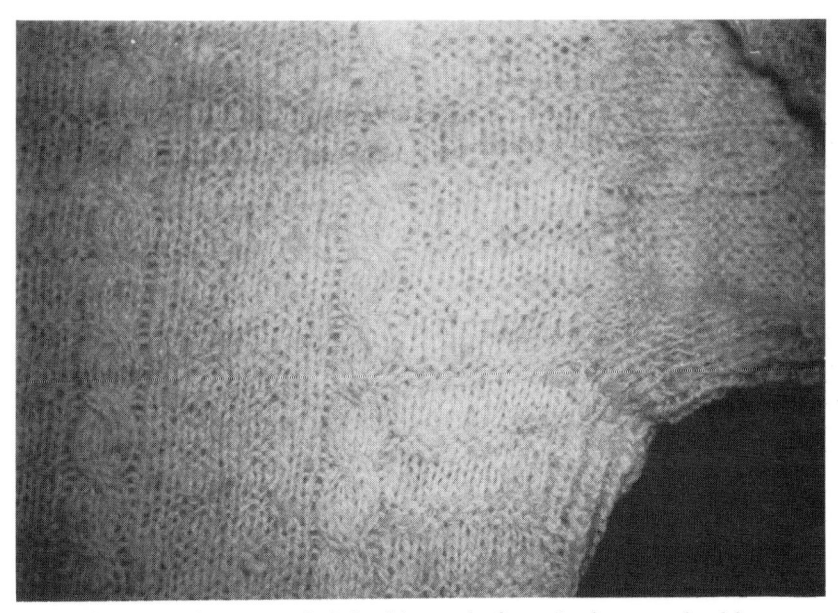

80. Close up of pattern. Original is made from 2 ply yarn double knitting-weight

fro. The shaping is much neater than stitched seams, particularly when different colours are joined in, for a striped pattern, and the flexible needle makes it easy to measure the work alongside a similar garment. (Ill. 89. 90)

A traditional Guernsey pattern, made of straight pieces without shaping, is very easily adapted once the tension has been worked out. The main pieces can be edged with ribbing or with garter stitch and the sleeves worked from the cuff, or knitted downwards on stitches picked up from the back and front, when they have been joined at the shoulder. (Ill. 79. 80)

Be sure to make the armhole deep enough — probably about 10 inches down from the shoulder — and if more room for movement is needed, make underarm gussets. In a traditional jersey these are knitted in with the main part, but they can be added later. Start with two stitches, and make increases every inch at each side until the gusset is the required width for under the arm, then make decreases at each side every inch until the stitches are used up. The long diamond shape is sewn in with the widest part under the arm and the points down the sleeve and between the back and front.

For a change, knit the main pieces sideways, so that contrasting stripes run up and down, instead of across. When casting on the stitches for back or front, this is not the total length. Stitches are picked up from the row ends to make the ribbing at the shoulder and at the waist. The shoulder ribbing is worked before stitches are picked up for the sleeves. The ribbing at the waist can be knitted last, when one side seam has been stitched up, and the front and back ribbing can be worked together. (Ill. 81, 82)

Some knitters like to work to a cut out pattern, rather than by counting rows in the usual way. If you try this, remember to allow a few inches "for ease", as with patterns for dressmaking, and cut the shapes in paper or firm fabric.

In designing a pattern, make sure there is room for the head to go through the neck ribbing. Constant stretching will put considerable strain on your spun yarn. With a fine or medium wool the neckband can be made double the finished length, then folded on to the inside, and the cast off stitches hemmed to the bottom edge of the ribbing. This makes a flexible edging, and avoids strain on cast off stitches.

A very heavy yarn would probably be too clumsy for a double neckband, so plan for a wide neckline, or use a finer wool for the ribbing.

81. *Jersey worked from side to side. Pattern based on simple rectangular shapes*

82. *Close up of pattern. Original used 2 thicknesses of soft spun 2 ply yarn (light weight)*

At the front the V neck starts just above the armholes. Count the stitches remaining on the back. Half that number will be gradually decreased at the neck edge of the front, probably every 3 or 4 rows.

When shaping the armholes cast off about 5 stitches at the beginning of the first 2 rows, then decrease one stitch at each end of alternate rows until the armhole shaping is complete.

Occasionally a garment does not work out according to plan, and as beginner's spinning can be difficult to unpick, starting all over again presents difficulties.

However, a rescue operation may be possible.

A neckband which proves rather tight to go over the head will keep its shape if botton-and-loop fastenings are added along the shoulder. This is the usual style for guernseys worn by Scottish fishermen. The loops can be worked in buttonhole stitch, or you can work double crochet along both edges, making chain stitch loops to fit the buttons.

If when it comes to the neck ribbing the neckline is wider and deeper than you had hoped, make the ribbing longer so that it fills in the space and becomes a yoke. Use a broad rib for a few inches (K3, P3, for instance) then reduce the stitches (to K3, P2, then K2 P2) to make the neckband fit. Continue in ribbing for a polo neck or finish as a flat round neckline.

If the pieces of a garment are too small, work an edging in crochet, along the side edges and around the armhole shaping, and round the sleeves if necessary, to make the extra inches you need.

A jersey made in "random" chunky spun yarn, with the pieces edged in a plain colour, looks as though you had planned it that way.

Another way of increasing the size is to add underarm gussets, reaching well down the sleeve and the main body of the jersey.

Sleeveless slipovers and tank tops are quickly made and easily designed. At their simplest they are made from two rectangles with some sort of firm edging stitch at the armholes, neckline and lower edge.

Make a sketch of the garment required, with measurements, and decide on the shape of the neckline-straight, round, U or V, for instance — and whether there is to be shaping at the armhole.

For a traditional slipover with V neck, the stitches on the back will be reduced by a quarter, or a little more, by the armhole shaping. One third of the remaining stitches will be cast off for each shoulder, and the rest of the stitches can be left on a spare needle for the neck ribbing.

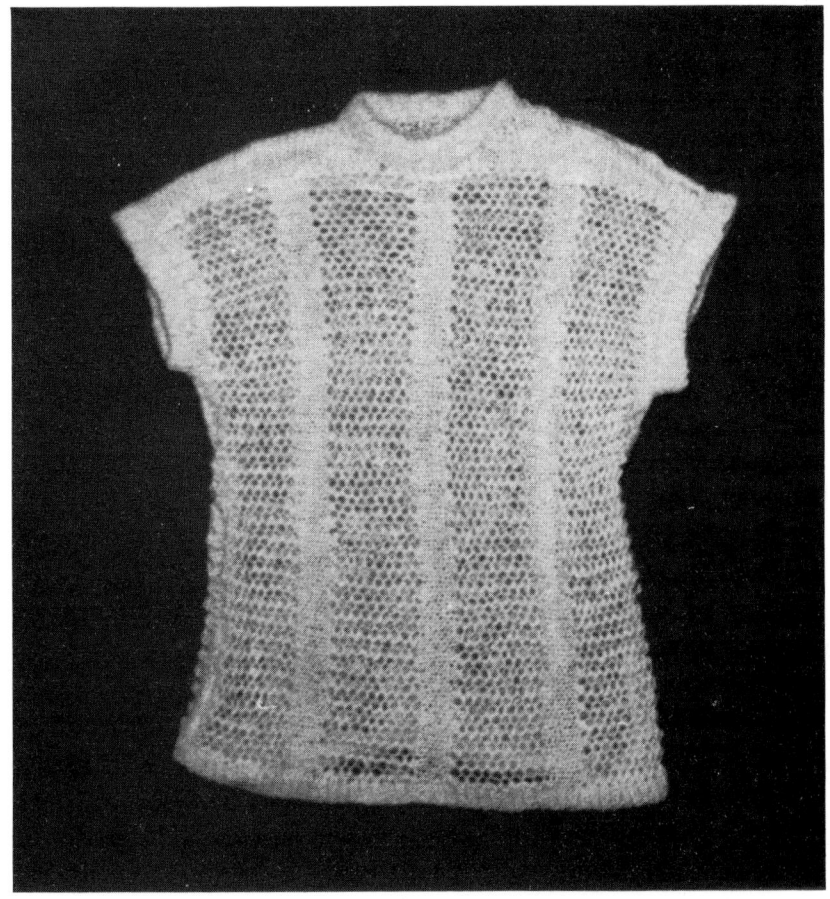

83. Simple top made from 4 oz lightweight 2 ply with button fastening on shoulder

Pick up stitches and knit ribbed bands with finer needles around the armholes and neck, and decrease one stitch each side of the centre stitch on each row to make the V on the front.

The slip-stitch pullover in illustration 84 made in two shades of grey, was made to the instructions for a 4-ply wool. The tension and measurements were exactly those of the pattern, but instead of using 10oz, as suggested in the pattern the pullover took only 7oz to make. Obviously the yarn is bulkier and lighter in comparison to the commercial version.

For a U shaped neckline, decide when the shaping should start — probably a few inches above the beginning of the armhole shaping — and leave the centre third of the "neck" stitches on a safety pin. Decrease at the neck edge one stitch on each row until just the "shoulder" stitches remain, then work straight to the shoulder. (Ill. 78)

A round neck is worked in a similar way, but begins about 3 inches short of the length of the back.

The sleeveless tops illustrated vary in weight from 4oz to 14oz, as they are made from very different types of yarn.

The drop shoulder top (Ill. 83) was knitted sideways, with a short shoulder yoke worked from picked-up stitches. The high round neck meant that the neck band had to be fastened with buttons and loops, as it was too narrow to go over the head. The ribbed bands on neck, armholes and lower edge are folded inside and hemmed to the first row of ribbing.

Specimen Pattern for Slipover in Heavy 2 ply yarn.

(Illustration 86)

This used 14oz heavy 2 ply worked at a tension of 3½ stitches and 5½ rows per inch on Size 5 needles.
Ribbing was worked on No. 7 needles.
Slipover fits size 38" to 40"..

Back

On No. 7 needles cast on 72 stitches.
1st Row K1 (K2 P2) to last 3 stitches, K3.
2nd Row K1 (P2 K2) to last 3 stitches, P2 K1.
Repeat these 2 rows until work measures 3 inches.
Change to No. 5 needles and broad rib pattern.
1st Row K3 (P2 K6) to last 5 stitches, P2 K3.
2nd Row K1, P2 (K2 P6) to last 5 stitches K2, P2, K1.
Repeat these two rows until work measures 16 inches from the beginning.

Shape armholes.

Cast off 5 stitches at beginning of each of next 2 rows.
Decrease each end of next and alternate rows until 46 stitches remain.
Work straight until work measures 25 inches from beginning then cast off 7 stitches at the beginning of each of the next 4 rows. Leave remaining 18 stitches on spare needle.

84. Sleeveless slipover in medium weight 2 ply Jacob

85. Close up of stitch

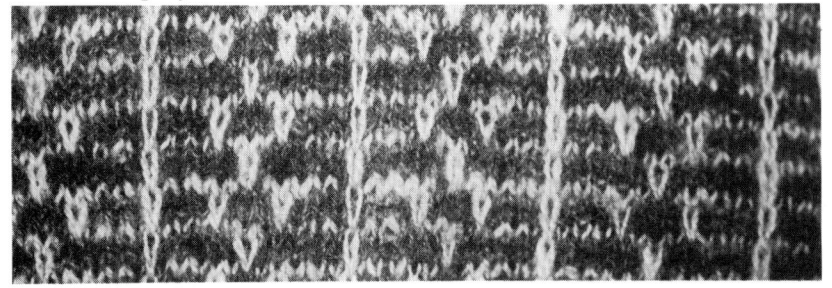

91

Front

As back until stitches are cast off at beginning of armhole shaping.
Next row. K2 together, work across next 27 stitches, K2 together.
Now join in another ball of wool to work across the other half of the front, and K2 together, work in pattern across 27 stitches. K2 together.

Remember to keep the 2 halves separate and continue shaping armholes and V neck, decreasing on the next 7 alternate rows on the armhole edge, and every fourth row at the neck edge, until 14 stitches remain at each side.

Continue until length matches back, then cast off 7 stitches at armhole edge at each side, then cast off the remaining 7 stitches from the armhole edge on each side.

Neck Ribbing

Place coloured thread or safety pin to mark centre of V-neck on front. Stitch right shoulder with back-stitch seam, then pick up, with No. 7 needle, 37 stitches evenly down left side of front neck, and 37 up right hand side, then work across the back neck stitches, P2, (K2 P2) 4 times.
Work back across all stitches in K2 P2 rib.
Now work 4 rows of rib, on each decreasing one stitch each side of the 2 Knit stitches in the centre of the front.
Cast off in rib.

Armhole ribbing

Stitch second shoulder. Pick up 80 stitches evenly on each armhole and work 6 rows in rib. Cast off in rib.
Join side seams.

86. *Slipover in chunky spun Jacob mixture*

How to plan a Raglan Pattern

To work out your own pattern, draw the shapes of the back, front, and sleeves, with body measurements. Add 2 inches to the width on the back, front, and upper arms.

Calculate the number of stitches required, after you have knitted a sample square to work out the tension.

Say, for instance, your tension is 4 stitches and 6 rows to an inch, and you want to knit a jersey for a 36" size. You will need to make the back and front each 20" wide, so cast on 20 × 4 stitches.

Armhole decreases are made at each end of alternate rows, until rather less than a third of the original stitches remain for the back of the neck.

The neck shaping on the front should begin after about two thirds of the armhole decreases have been worked. Leave the middle third of the neck stitches on a safety pin, and decrease at each side of the neck and at the armhole edges on alternate rows, until the stitches are used up, and the length of the front matches the back.

When calculating the number of stitches for the top of the sleeve, before beginning the raglan shaping, count the number of decreases on the back and front. There must be enough stitches on the sleeve to complete those decreases and to leave a few stitches at the base of the neckband.

The wrist needs rather more than half the stitches required for the back. When the ribbing is completed increase each end of every 6th row until the full number of stitches are on the needle. This should bring the sleeve to its full width a few inches below the armhole.

Sleeve decreases are worked as for the back.

Pick up stitches down each side of the neck at the front, and, making sure they are assembled in the right order, work ribbing on stitches left on the front, back and sleeves.

For a V-neck the neck shaping at the front begins at the same time as the raglan shaping, decreasing at the neck edge every 4th row until the neck stitches are used up. When working the neck ribbing, decrease at centre front to make the V-neckline.

Obviously the amount of wool required varies according to thickness and type, and the size of needles used, as well as the size of the garment. The lacy patterned 34" size jersey in Illustration 87 is made of 6oz of a soft lustrous 2-ply, whereas one family favourite raglan jersey weighs 2lb.

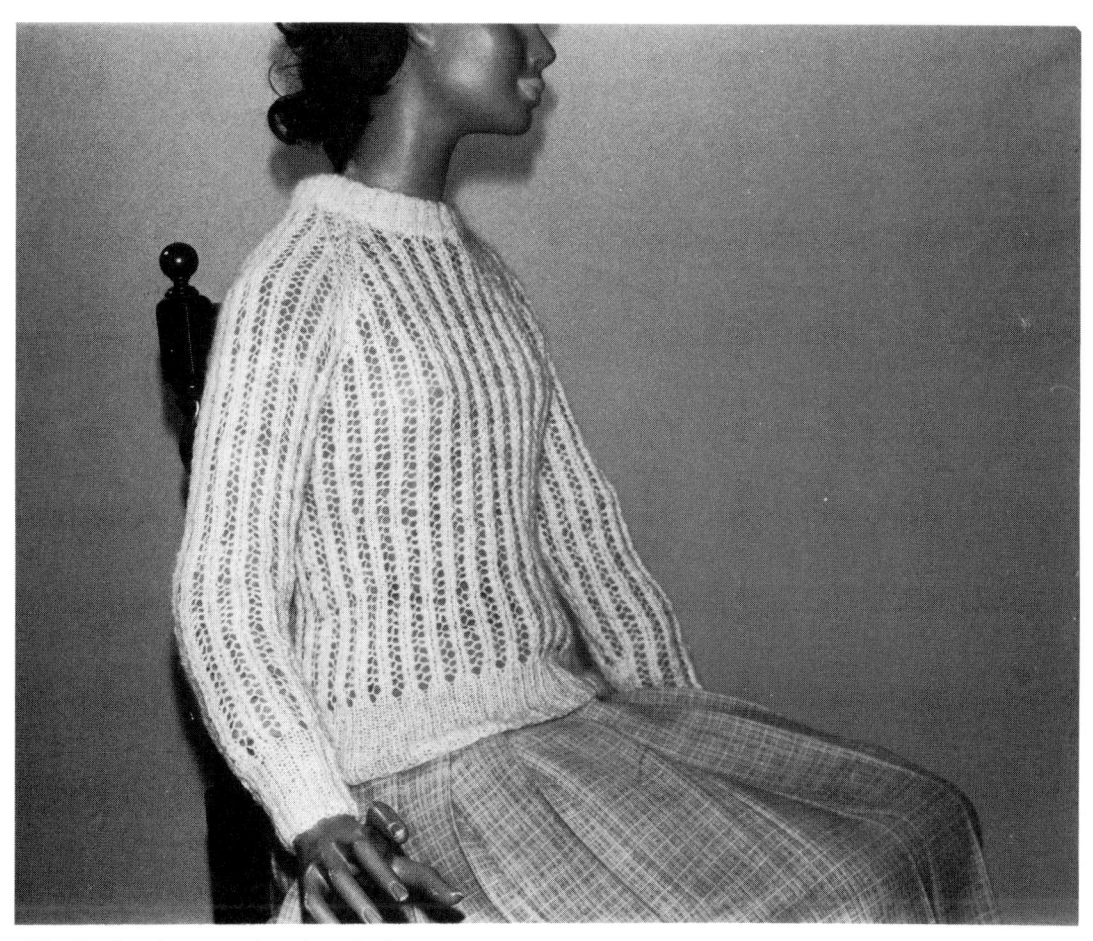

87. *Raglan jersey using 6 oz 2 ply Romney*

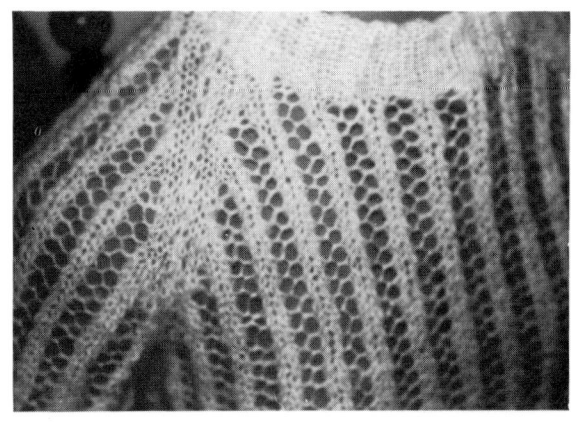

88. *Close up of simple lace pattern*

For a cardigan, or high necked raglan jacket, remember to allow extra stitches for the button and buttonhole bands. Otherwise the shaping is similar to a jersey. The front bands can be worked along with the fronts (both worked together, to save the difficulty of counting rows to match) or bands can be added afterwards, picking up stitches down the edge of the front and knitting sideways for the required width, making buttonholes evenly spaced along the row half way through the width of the band. The button band is knitted to match, omitting buttonholes.

Specimen Raglan Pattern

This used 18oz medium heavy 2 ply, worked at a tension of 4 stitches and 6 rows per inch on size 6 needles.

Actual measurement 40″ for 36″ size.

This is just for guidance. Adjust as necessary.

Back

Cast on 80 stitches on size 8 needles. Rib K2 P2 for 3 inches.
Change to size 6 needles.
Work straight to armholes, (original was K6 P2 rib, arranged with a 'P2' in the centre), 15 inches or desired length.
Cast off one stitch at the beginning of the next 2 rows.
Now decrease each end of the next and alternate rows — K1, K2 together through back loops, pattern to last 3 sts, K2 tog, K1. Work next row in pattern without shaping, purling first 2 and last 2 stitches.
Repeat these 2 rows until 24 stitches remain and leave these on a stitch holder for neck ribbing.

Front

As back until 44 stitches remain.
On next row place centre 10 stitches on safety pin.
Join in a second ball of wool so that both halves of the front can be knitted together, and continue decreasing on alternate rows on armhole edges, at the same time knitting 2 together at the neck edge on alternate rows, until last 2 stitches are knitted together at each side of neck shaping.

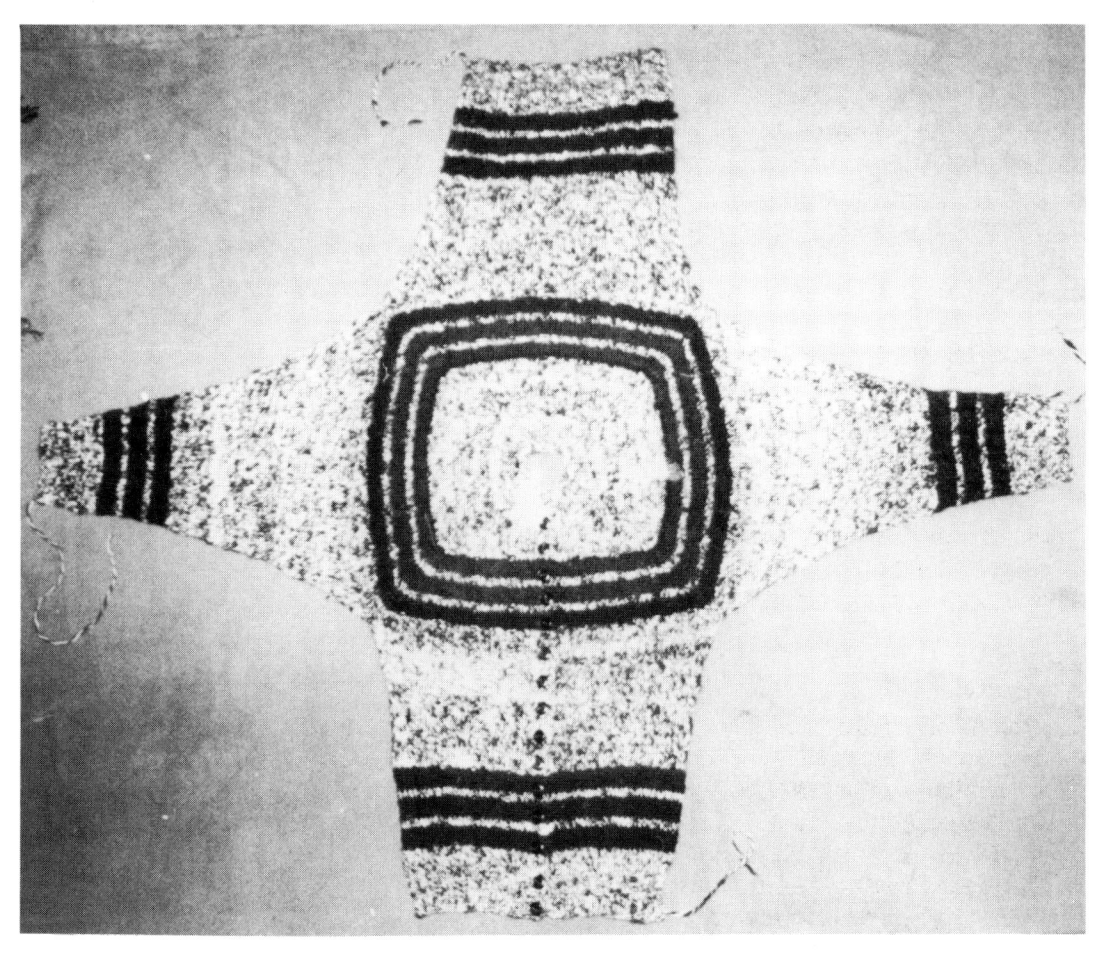

89. Raglan button-up before stitching side and sleeve seams

Sleeves (both alike)

Cast on 44 stitches on No. 8 needles. Work 3 inches in rib, increasing in last row to 48 stitches.

Change to Size 6 needles and pattern, increasing each end of every 6th row to 72 stitches.

Continue to 18 inches (or desired length) then decrease as for back until 16 stitches remain, leave on spare needle.

Neck ribbing

With size 8 needle work K1, P2 (K2 P2) 3 times, K1, across left sleeve stitches, pick up 13 stitches down left side of neck, P2, K2, P2, K2, P2 on stitches from safety pin, pick up 13 stitches up right side of neck, K1, P2 (K2 P2) 3 times, K1 across right sleeve stitches. K1, P2 (K2 P2) 5 times, K1 on back neck stitches.
Continue ribbing K2 P2 for 3 inches, then cast off loosely.
Block and press, then stitch seams and hem cast off edge of neck ribbing to first row of ribbing on inside.

90. Raglan in Jacob wool-2 ply of double knitting weight

Stoles and Shawls

Long stoles are easier to design than square shawls, as there is no corner shaping to worry about. Borders can be worked at each side along with the main part, or they can be added later. If you crochet, work a crochet border on your knitted shawl. There are some very pretty traditional patterns for knitted lace edgings, too. One of these borders on a plainly knitted stole makes it a very exclusive item.

A simple lacy stitch, very useful for scarves, shawls and stoles, is known variously as Purse Stitch, Chain Mail Stitch and Mock Turkish Stitch. Have an even number of stitches, and work every row the same:-

Wool round needle to make 1, Purl 2 together
Repeat from * to * across the row.

This stitch stretches in both directions, so if the fringe is made too heavy in proportion to the weight of the stole, it will stretch into a very long stole indeed!

Attractive soft spun yarns make cosy, warm looking scarves and stoles in simple garter stitch — every row knit. Use fairly large needles, and make a few sample squares so that you can choose the tension which show off the wool best.

Thick wool "goes further" if knitted with rows of elongated stitches at regular intervals — every eighth or tenth row for instance. On that row wrap the yarn round the needle three times for each stitch. On the following row knit, dropping the extra loops.

Knitted shawls need very little planning as measurements do not have to be exact. Check the tension on a sample, and use a bought pattern, or make your own design.

The centre part of a square shawl can be knitted first, in garter stitch, moss stitch, or a simple lace stitch, and the stitches picked up on each side to make the border, increasing at the ends of the rows to make the corners fit. Faggoting makes a softer join than ordinary seaming for completing the corners.

If you enjoy knitting on a set of needles, or a circular needle, knit a shawl from the centre outwards. Use five needles rather than four for a square shawl, so that increases are worked at each end of the needle. By the time the shawl has grown sufficiently to use a circular needle the increase points should be easy to find. Mark one corner to show when the round begins.

Cast on 8 stitches, place 2 on each of 4 needles, and on alternate rounds work 8 increases, one at each end of each needle. The first few rounds are admittedly, very "fiddly", but by the time there are twelve stitches on each needle the work is very simple. Choose your stitch — wavy lace patterns look good in fine wool — and introduce it when there is room for a repeat between the increases.

A circular shawl can also be worked from the centre outwards, but here the increases are evenly spaced, instead of making them at the ends of the needles and a little more planning is needed to keep the circle flat.

Sometimes a soft shawl is spoiled by the tight casting off around the edge. Avoid this by casting off with a crochet hook. Work a double crochet through the first three stitches from the needle, then make a loop of chain stitches before taking off the next three stitches with a double crochet. The chain loop can be just long enough to reach comfortably to the next group of stitches, or a little longer, to make a lacy edging.

To make a fine Shetland Shawl in the traditional manner, with no long cast on or cast off edges, refer to Mary Thomas's Knitting Book, a mine of information!

FACING PAGE

91. Long stole in light weight 2 ply knitted in purse stitch with crochet border

101

Crochet and other ideas

Even the crudest of rough spun yarn becomes presentable with the aid of a crochet hook and a little planning.

The hook size must be suited to the thickness of the wool and the article being made.

Hats and mittens need very little skill, and will use up the relatively small quantities of "experimental" spinning.

If your tension is right, follow a commercial pattern, but even at a different tension it is easy to adapt a hat pattern, once the method is understood.

For a simple crochet hat, work in rounds, starting from the crown. Use heavy singles or two threads of finer wool, and work in half trebles to make a firm fabric. Make an almost flat circle for the crown of the hat, then work straight to the required depth. To add a brim increase in every other stitch then work a few more rounds for the brim. Either in a plain colour or a tweedy mixture, your hat will prove to be an indispensable weather beater, the envy of your friends! A hat band in finger weaving will give it the final rouch. (Ill. 92)

If you have enough of it, use your chunky-spun for a crochet knee-rug. This should not be as "solid" as the hat. Work a sample to decide on the hook size and the stitch. Aim at making a soft, flexible fabric, in rows of trebles, shells, or double trebles, or a heavy version of fillet crochet, alternating blocks and spaces. As with any project using beginner's spinning with a homespun look, simple patterns are the most effective.

Squares and Oblongs

Patterns based on squares, starting from the middle and increasing in each corner, are easily adapted for cushion covers and cot or pram covers.

To make an oblong, rather than square shape, start by making a length of chain. Work along the chain, making increases at the end, then work along the other side of the chain, making increases at the starting point. From here work in rounds with corner increases, as when making a square. (Ill. 93)

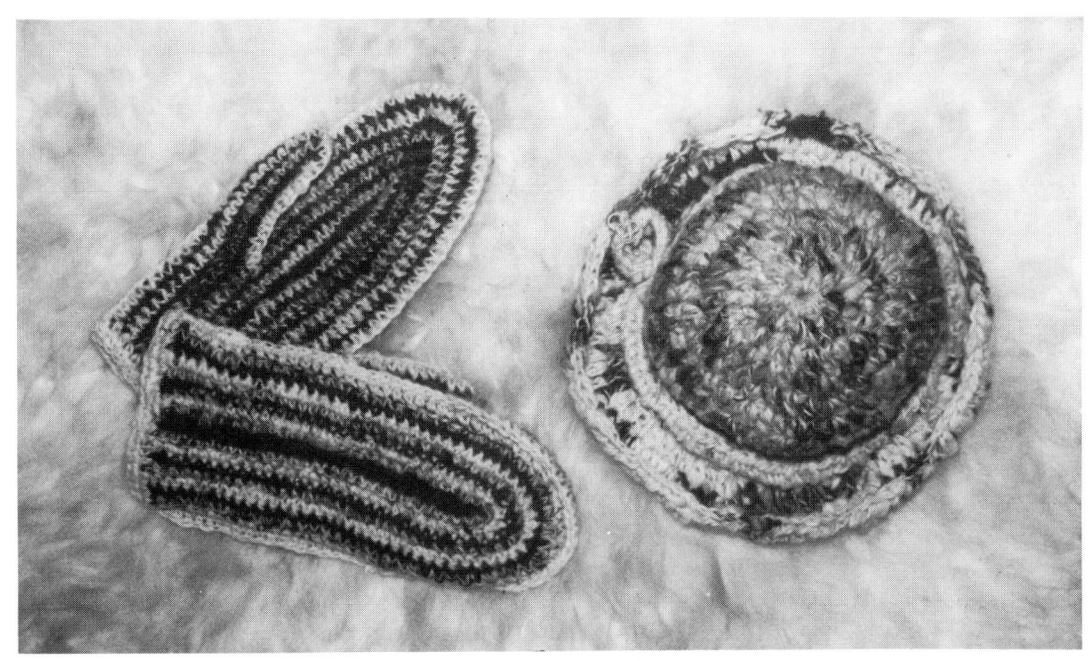

92. *Crochet hat in heavy handspun*
    mittens in medium weight yarn

93. *Soft spun plied yarn was used for*
    this simple cot cover

Medallion Crochet

A collection of crochet medallion patterns will offer inspiration for using handspun of all weights. Make sure the sections can be joined together as they are made. Sewing them together is tedious, and if two squares are held back to back and joined with double crochet, as suggested in some pattern books, there will be a hard ridge which spoils the look and feel of the work. It should be possible to link the sections together as the last round of each piece is being worked. A slip stitch join is made at any point in the pattern where the squares meet, at the corners and along the side; this makes work look "whole" rather than a collection of bits.

Square, triangular and hexagonal motifs fit together well. Between circular medallions there will be spaces which may need to be filled with small joining motifs — probably small circles with chain loops connecting to the larger medallions.

The advantage of medallion crochet is that a final decision on the dimensions can be left until a project is well on its way. After finding how many motifs can be made from one ounce you can decide whether you are making a shoulder shawl, a poncho, or a long stole.

Motif crochet can be used for blouses and sleeveless tops as well as the more usual shawls.

Draw a plan of the garment to be made, work out how the medallions should be arranged, and mark off on your plan each section as it is worked, so that when you next pick it up you can make sense of the unfinished shape.

Using yarn of different weights, the same patterns can be used for rugs, heavy shawls and ponchos, or for very lightweight shawls and blouses.

If the squares are set diagonally, you may need some half squares, too. Even if the instructions do not describe how this can be done, it is very simple to work out. Draw your square and divide it diagonally. The centre of the square now becomes the middle of the long side, so start there and work a corner, two sides, and another corner. Instead of going on to work 2 more sides, finish off at that corner, and rejoin at the first corner to work on the two sides only.

Irish crochet, with roses worked in relief on a diamond picot background, is equally suitable for fine or medium weight yarns. The shawl in Illustration 94 is roughly triangular, based on a pattern of squares. The long side is about 64", and with fairly fine singles (about 300 yds per oz) the shawl, including its heavy fringe, took less than 4oz.

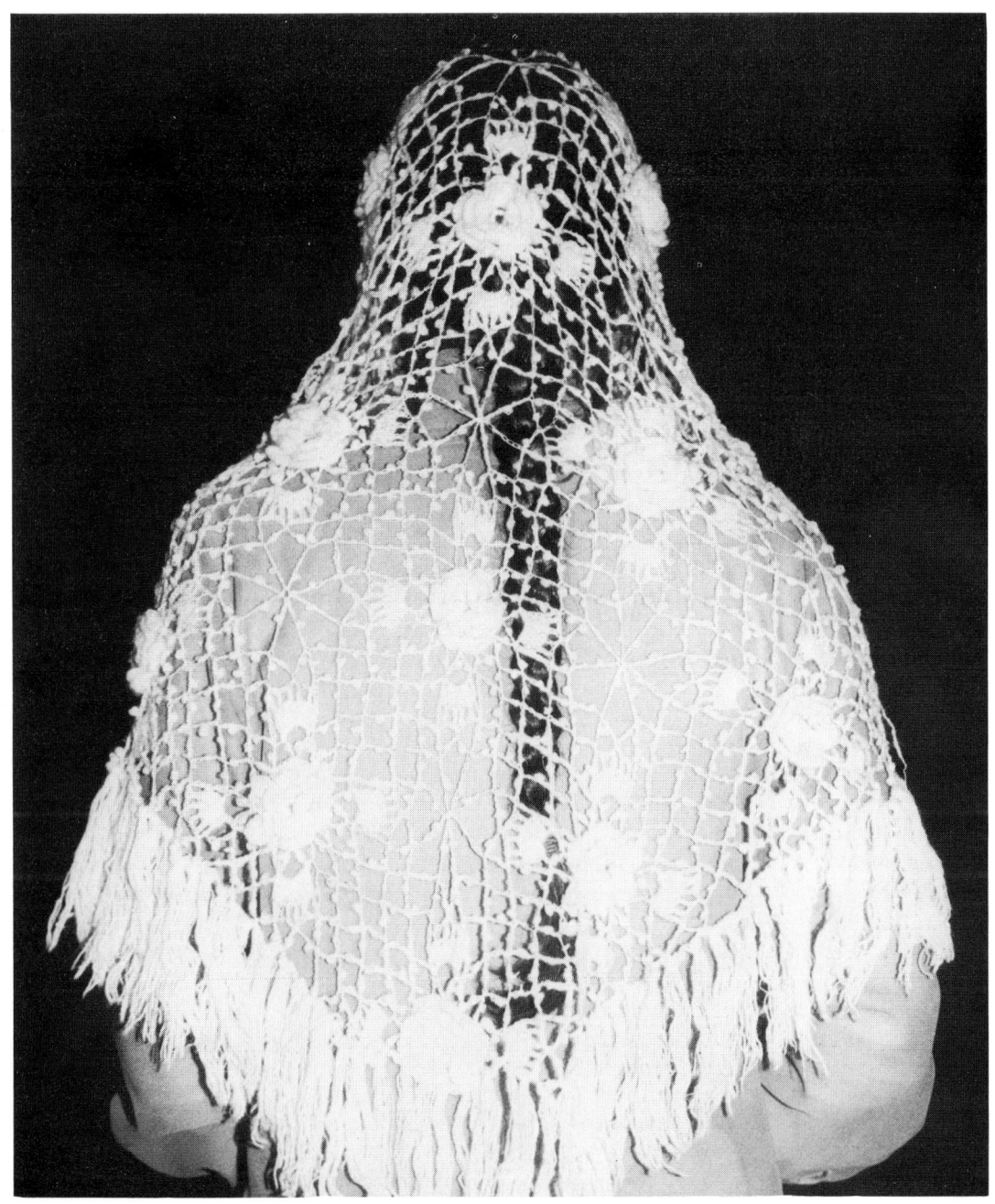

94. *Irish Crochet shawl*

A very simple motif pattern was used for the shawl in Illustration 95. The "flowers" were worked in shades of brown, made by blending dark and light Jacob wool in different proportions, and the final round of each motif, the "joining" round, was worked in plain cream Jacob wool from the same fleece. Four ounces of fairly fine wool makes a large shawl.

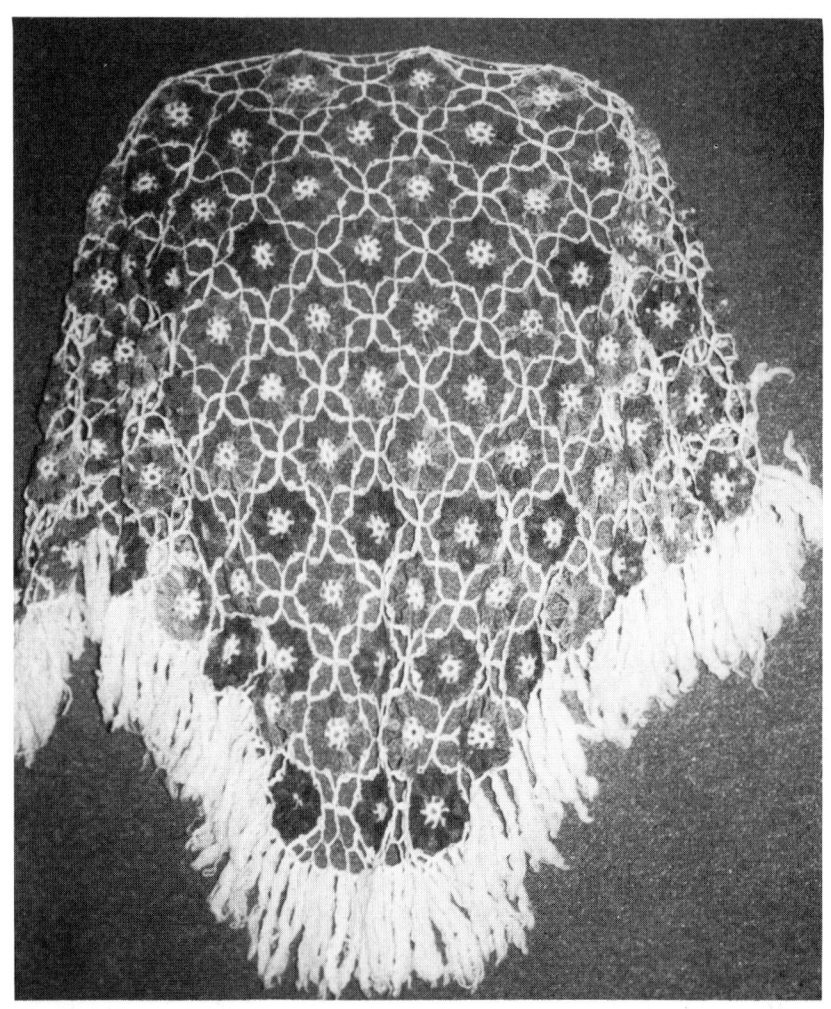

95. *Jacob wool shawl in simple medallion pattern*

Long Stoles

The long stole on the right in Illustration 96 was made with a fine singles from a Gotland fleece, and weighs less than 2oz. The pale silvery grey yarn has an attractive sheen, and a simple pattern of blocks and spaces was chosen, as the wool needs no further ornament. This was a delightful fleece to spin, and although it is soft and fine it washes easily without the worries of shrinking and felting associated with many soft wools.

The same fleece was used for the stole on the left in Illustration 96, but this time the yarn was plied. The simple medallion pattern is finished off with a border of treble crochet.

It is very easy to adapt a design as you go along. Perhaps you start making a scarf of medium width, and the yarn goes much further than you expected. There is enough wool to work borders along the sides of the scarf, to make it into a generous sized stole.

Often the weight of a fringe improves the "hang" of a shawl, as well as showing off your handspun yarn.

96. Two stoles made of Gotland yarn

Further Crochet Ideas

A strong, hardwearing yarn, made into a firm fabric in simple crochet is ideal for chair or stool seats; fitting and shaping are particularly easy with crochet work.

Floor rugs are a possibility, too, for anyone who would rather use a crochet hook than a loom. Use strong thick threads, or several together, with a large hook. There are crochet looped stitches, to make a rug with a "pile", and it is a simple matter to make your rug to whatever shape you need.

For cardigans, jackets and waistcoats, use yarn of medium weight. If the tension is right follow a bought pattern, or you can devise your own, following the shape of a favourite garment, or working to a cut-out pattern.

The jacket shown in Illustration 97 was made of all the odds and ends of yarns left over from a number of projects. It was worked from the top downwards, making the yoke all in one; the fronts and the back were worked together, and the sleeves worked in rounds. The yarns used varied, so they were used two or three together to achieve a fairly uniform thickness. The button and buttonhole bands were worked last, and the remaining oddments of wool were used to crochet covers for the buttons. The resulting garment has lasted for years, although admittedly it is now past its best!

Other Uses for Handspun Yarns

Even without a loom you can make "pile" rugs with suitably strong handspun yarn. Use an old-fashioned latchet hook and rug canvas, and as many thicknesses of wool as seems suitable to get the effect you need — solid or "shaggy" pile.

Use your handspun yarns for making toys. They may be knitted and stuffed with washed fleece, or built up from a collection of woolly balls made by winding wool on card shapes, and making pom-poms. With a little ingenuity in the blending of colours of fleece you will make some very attractive animals.

Anyone who likes to make three-dimensional "soft sculptures" will find endless inspiration to make and use interesting yarns.

Handspun yarns for embroidery, especially soft-spun wool for couching, give scope for great originality in shade and texture.

Whatever craft you enjoy, if threads are used your work can be even more interesting when you spin your own yarns.

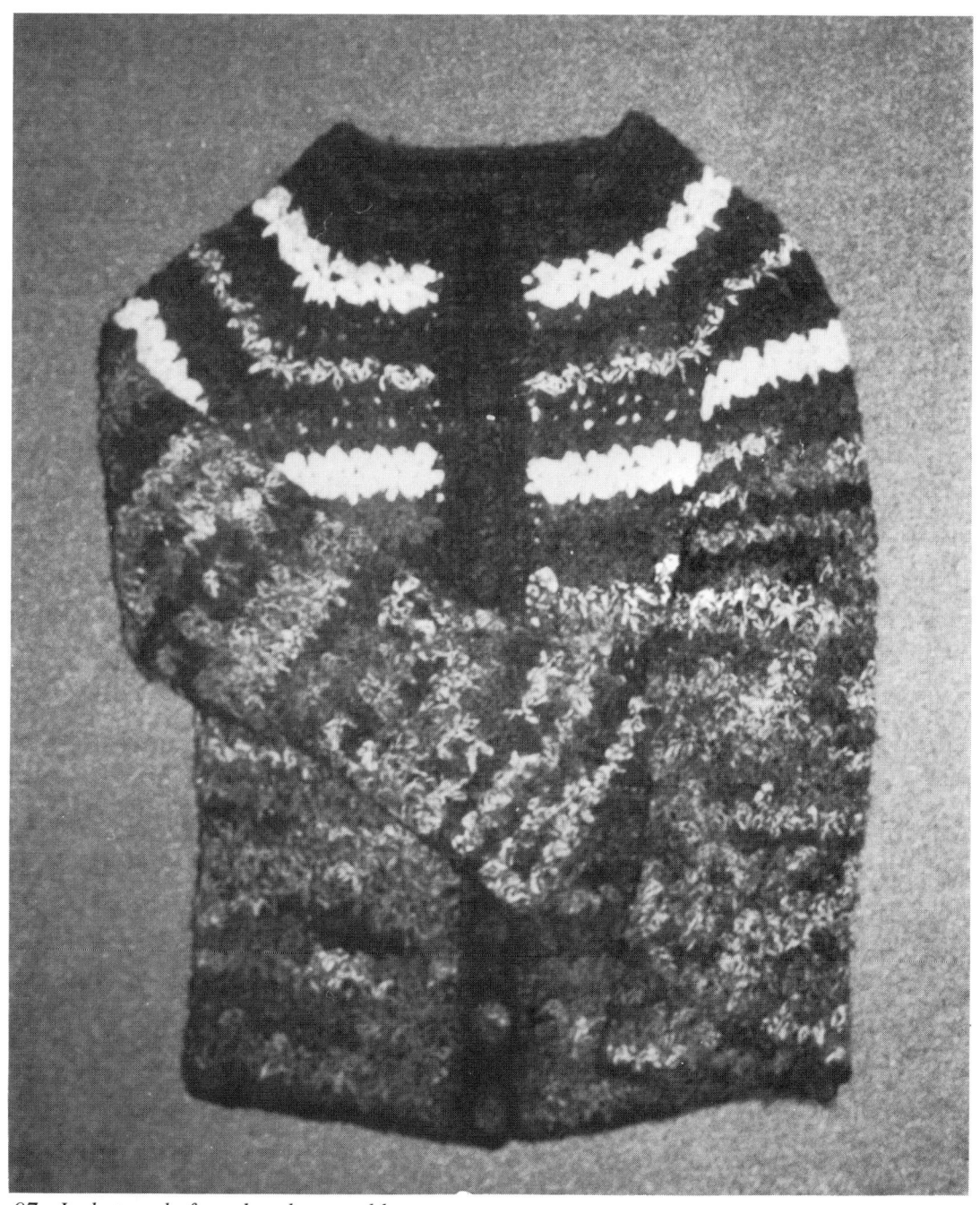

97. Jacket made from handspun oddments

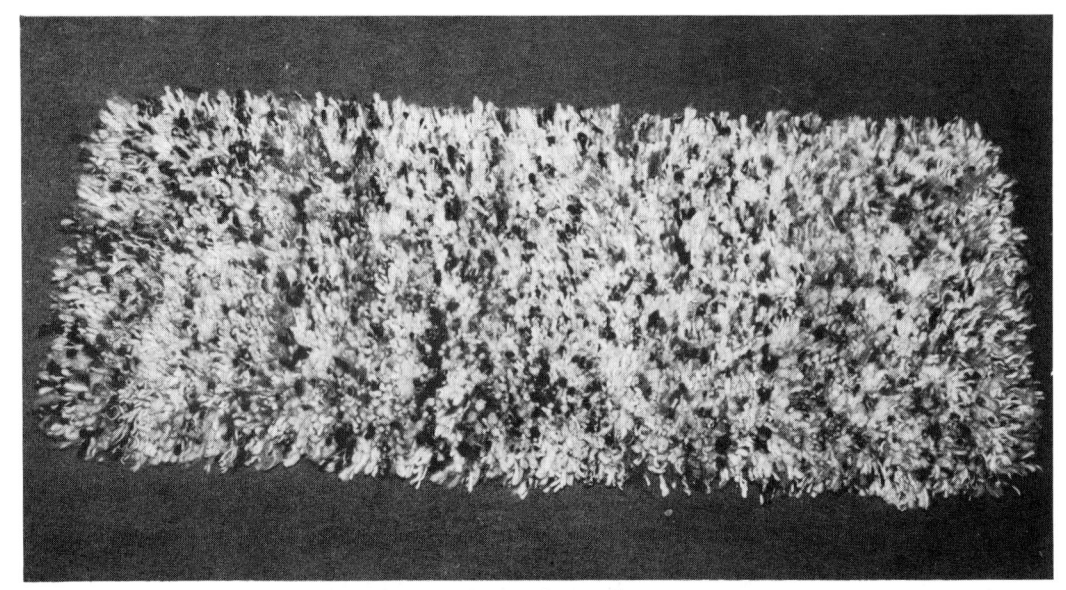

98. Hooked rug worked on canvas with Jacob wool

99. Close up of rug

Some Useful Books.

Spinning Wheels, Spinners and Spinning.
Patricia Baines. Batsford, London 1977

Hand Woolcombing and Spinning.
Peter Teal. Blandford Press. Poole Dorset 1976.

Fleece in Your Hands.
Beverley Horne. Interweave Press. Loveland Colorado 1979.

Patterns for Guernseys, Jerseys and Arans.
Gladys Thompson. Dover Publications Inc. New York 1971.

Mary Thomas's Knitting Book.
Hodder & Stoughton Ltd, London 1938.
Republished Dover Publications Inc. New York (Paperback)
Peter Smith. Magnolia Mass. (Hardback)

Mary Thomas's Book of Knitting Patterns.
Hodder and Stoughton 1943.

British Sheep Breeds, their wool and its uses.
British Wool Marketing Board, Oak Mills, Clayton, Bradford,
West Yorkshire BD14 6JD. 1984.

British Wool Fleeces

The following range of fleeces have been specially selected by the British Wool Marketing Board to cover a wide range of hand-spinning requirements.

Type No	Description	Average Staple Length	Count	Handle	Colour	Approximate Weight of Normal Greasy Fleece
84226	Fine Wool White	3-4″	56's	Soft	White	2-3 Kilos
84291	Fine Wool Dark	3-4″	56's	Soft	Grey/Black	2-3 Kilos
84308	Romney (Kent)	4-5″	50-54's	Medium	White	3-4 Kilos
84322	Leicester Cheviot Cross	6-7″	50-54's	Soft/Medium	White	3-4 Kilos
84350	Jacobs	5-6″	50-56's	Soft	Piebald	1½-2½ Kilos
84413	Masham	4-6″	46-48's	Medium/Harsh	White	2-3 Kilos
84491	Masham Dark	4-6″	46-50's	Medium/Harsh	Dark Grey	2-3 Kilos
84603	Cheviot	3-5″	54-56's	Soft	White	2-3 Kilos
84691	Welsh Black	2-3″	48-56's	Soft/Medium	Black	1-2 Kilos
84221	Fine Hog Wool White	4-5″	56's	Soft	White	2-3 Kilos

A GUIDE TO USE

Staple Length

2″	staple	—	for the experienced spinner suitable for woollen spinning
3″ - 4″	staple	—	recommended for beginners suitable for woollen spinning
5″ - 7″	staple	—	recommended for beginners suitable for worsted spinning
Over 7″	staple	—	better suited to the experienced spinner

Qualities

Soft to medium	—	suitable for spinning apparel fabrics
Medium to harsh	—	suitable for tweeds, coat and upholstery fabrics
Harsh	—	suitable for upholstery and floorcoverings

Reproduced by courtesy of the British Wool Marketing Board,

112

Glossary

Batt	— mass of aligned fibres prepared on drum carders.
Butt	— shorn end of wool.
Carding	— aligning fibres on carders for making rolags.
Count	— quality number; the higher the number the finer the fleece.
Crimp	— natural waves in wool.
Drafting	— drawing out fibres from rolag for spinning.
Drawing in	— yarn winding onto bobbin.
Drive ratio	— relation between diameters of drive wheel and spindle whorl, which determines number of revolutions of flyer for each beat on the treadle.
Felting	— matting of fibres (by a combination of moisture, heat and friction) into a solid mass which cannot be parted for spinning. Felt is the fabric which is deliberately made by pounding together layers of previously wetted fibres.
Grease	— natural oils in wool. Unwashed wool is "in the grease".
Inkle weaving	— method of weaving narrow bands on a simple, portable loom, an inkle loom.
Kemp	— short, brittle, chalky white fibres, common in the wool of hill sheep.
Leader	— length of yarn tied to bobbin and led through orifice. Yarn is spun onto leader.
Lustre	— natural sheen, typical of longwools.
Niddy-noddy	— simple implement for winding skeins.
Noils	— small tufts and knots discarded during preparation of fleece
Orifice	— eye in metal spindle shaft through which yarn is led onto bobbin.
Plying	— twisting two or more single yarns to make a thicker thread. Plied yarns give much better results than singles for knitted garmets.
Rolag	— spiral of carded wool, trapping air, for wool spinning.
Rooed	— plucked (wool) instead of being shorn.
Scotch tension	— braking device on bobbin of single drive band wheel.
Shearling	— sheep shorn for the first time, just over a year old, also called hogg, hogget and teg.

Singles	— yarn which is not plied.
Sliver	— fibres prepared and drawn out but not twisted.
Sorting	— separating fleece into different grades.
Staple	— tuft or lock of wool.
S-twist	— anticlockwise spin on yarn.
Tablet weaving	— method of weaving narrow bands with the warp threaded through holes in the corners of cards, or tablets. Pattern is made by turning the cards to re-arrange the warp threads before inserting the weft.
Teasing	— separating fibres of locks of wool so that they lie parallel.
Tentering	— drying completed woven and washed fabric on an adjustable frame (a tenter frame) where the cloth is stretched onto hooks (tenterhooks) so that it dries in the correct shape.
Whorl	— weight on hand spindle; pulley on spindle shaft of wheel.
Woollen yarn	— yarn spun from carded wool.
Worsted yarn	— yarn spun from combed wool.
Z-twist	— ciockwise — spun yarn.